The Nimble Negotiator

Beat negotiation at its own game

Juliet Erickson

First published in the USA in 2014 by Juliet Erickson
Provideo Press
San Francisco, California

© 2014 Juliet Erickson

ISBN-13: 9781495365058
ISBN-10: 1495365050
Library of Congress Control Number: 2014902035
CreateSpace Independent Publishing Platform
North Charleston, South Carolina

For Peter

Wanderer, there is no path. The path is made by walking.

Antonio Machado

Contents

Acknowledgments

Heartfelt gratitude to my editor, Caroline Taggart for her calm, charm, and great talent; my colleagues Dr. Mark Schmid-Neuhaus and Christine Agnello for their support and friendship; and my clients and students who have contributed in every way.

Introduction

Negotiation is part of everyone's life on some level – student to CEO. It may be with a partner or colleague, a family member or a stranger. It may be important or trivial, formal or informal, simple or complex.

You may be smart, creative, and great at what you do for a living; you may be a loving and caring individual, sensitive and intuitive, respected and wise. Yet – like most of the rest of us – you are probably uncomfortable with negotiating and don't know how to do it well.

Negotiating can be a bit of an enigma wrapped up in fear and dipped in mystery sauce. The discomfort you feel puts you at a disadvantage – it takes away your power. It needn't be that way. I think you can beat negotiating at its own game.

How? By practicing and seeking clarity.

Like any mystery, take away the unknown and you see it for what it is. Like any fear, face it and it gradually disappears. Clarity is a great equalizer.

Seeking clarity is demanding and uncomfortable work and evades most negotiators. However, the benefits to you and the people with whom you negotiate are palpable.

The Nimble Negotiator offers a way to turn a challenge into an opportunity. You will learn the most important skills and tools (gathered from my years of working with the best and worst negotiators) that you need to make negotiating a more effective, natural, and pleasant experience. These skills are powerful enough to use in your toughest situations yet adaptable enough to work in day-to-day give and take with friends and family.

In the book, you will find:

- Proven tips and guidelines on how to plan and prepare for any negotiation.
- Tools to help you demystify the negotiating process by identifying the dynamics involved.
- A greater understanding of the impact of your actions and reactions during a negotiation, and their effect on the outcome.
- Ways to use the key face-to-face communication skills that will help you support your relationships when you negotiate.

As a result, you will understand, and have greater influence over, each part of a negotiation, leading to more successful outcomes overall.

I've included examples and tips, drawn from my personal and professional life as well as from my involvement in training and coaching the practice of negotiation for over 20 years. In addition, my clients, students, colleagues, friends, and fellow travelers have shared their wisdom with me. I am now privileged to pass it on to you, to guide you on your way to becoming a Nimble Negotiator.

Enjoy.

one

Are We Negotiating?

Ah, what a dusty answer gets the soul when hot for certainties in this life.
George Meredith

Negotiation skills are the most sought-after courses at business schools around the world. Check out the bestseller lists and a negotiation book will likely be on it. Mention the word negotiation and you'll get different physical reactions and points of view ranging from fear to fun, and epic stories of success and failure.

Yet most people don't know when they are negotiating and, when they are, don't know how to do it very well.

I like to think about negotiation in simple terms. It is nothing more than communication in search of agreement over who gets what. There is naturally some fear and tension around how things are going to turn out. Unfortunately, this fear and tension is stoked by the modern hyperbole of negotiation.

This is the essence of how *The Nimble Negotiator* came to be.

The key difference between a Nimble Negotiator and everyone else? The Nimble Negotiator brings effective communication to the negotiating table.

For decades well-meaning and scholarly advice has been written about negotiation. How to achieve "win-win" or "win-lose", hard-ball bargaining, interest-based, value-based, relationship-based, rigid and extensive planning and processes that have made negotiation seem a little complicated, out of step with, and not easy to translate into, everyday work and life.

We know now that rigid, linear, one-size-fits-all rules just don't work in real-world negotiation. There is too much in flux. There are a lot of demands on our attention. Information and insight are available more quickly and easily than they were say 20 years ago. Different demands are made from more varied business and personal relationships. Goals change. Stories change. Temperaments change.

It is also now fairly commonplace for people to negotiate with others from around the world. My clients in California, for example, routinely negotiate with lawyers or colleagues from London, Mumbai, Geneva, Moscow, and Shanghai. Now, any cultural complexities or differences are closer than ever. Not only do we have culture outside work, but company or group cultures start to take shape. Also, most of this communication is over the phone or via tele-conference, making clarity and understanding harder to achieve. Even video-conferencing has its limitations. Contextual cues (facial expression, body language, tone of voice) are missing or distorted, so the messages you send and receive are different from what they would be if you were there in person. So much of what we mean is transmitted by these cues. Without them, messages and meaning can get muddled more easily.

So, enter communication. In all this clutter, it is natural to mistake the need to negotiate with a simple need to communicate effectively.

What is negotiation?

The very word negotiation seems to compel people to respond by gearing up for a fight. Jumping into what you only *think* is a negotiation can result in disagreements that go on too long, disappointments due to outcomes that don't meet expectations, frustration, confusion, and miscommunication. You can create the need for a negotiation when there isn't one. Negotiation itself often begets negotiation.

Many people believe they are "negotiating all the time" and every day, with family, friends, strangers, and colleagues. Frankly, the idea of this exhausts me and I don't believe it is true. I don't think we (need to) negotiate as often as we think we do.

The conventional belief that you are negotiating "all the time" means you have stopped listening. You bring a mindset to the day-to-day business of getting along with other people and the sorting out of differences that could mean you react before you understand. Too much effort goes into managing your guesses or clarifying a position after the fact. This often puts you at a disadvantage.

Each term at the beginning of class I ask my students to be prepared to discuss an example of negotiations in which they are currently or regularly engaged so we can work on aspects of it "live". Interestingly, I find with a little probing that most of the initial examples I receive are not necessarily negotiation situations. They include internal budgeting or resource proposals, job seeking and salary reviews, new business pitches, fee discussions, funding proposals, and disputes with family members, to name a few.

All of these activities could certainly require you to negotiate at some stage, but are not in and of themselves a prompt for a negotiation! Often people think they are negotiating when actually they would be better off doing something else: for example, presenting, pitching or discussing, declaring, asking, arguing, probing, confronting, clarifying, handling an objection, or some other persuasive communication activity.

Many of us are engaged in what we believe to be on-going negotiations with colleagues, friends, family, or clients but are not clear about the other party's understanding, expectations, or objectives. This is a common problem because people do proceed into what they think is a negotiation, or go into "negotiation mode", without considering if this is the right thing to do. Before you negotiate salary, have you been offered the job? Before you negotiate fees, does the client understand that you can solve their problem and do they know *how* you can solve it? Before you negotiate with your nagging teenager, is it really a negotiation? Do they have a choice? Before you negotiate what you want, are you clear about what you can get? Before you negotiate with your spouse about sharing the household chores, do you have a clear idea about how they see things?

Here are some criteria to use to determine if you are negotiating:

- You are negotiating if there is more than one issue at stake. Issues are more than money or price. They can be something specific like date of delivery or something much less easy to know or define, like personal principles or beliefs. People often value issues differently and they are specific to a negotiation context. An issue is whatever you think it is.

- If there is only one issue, it's considered a haggle. People can quibble over small things. It is a sport for some people and a horror for others. My husband would rather be overcharged than haggle over the price.

The value of communication

Asking and clarifying – communicating – goes the longest way toward ending bargaining from opposite corners and focusing on problem solving. Research shows us that more often than not in the top three lessons learned from hostage and high-stakes negotiation is the belief that if there had been better communication between the parties at the start, much of the time and trouble would have been averted.

The importance of good communication, asking and clarifying early and often, is demonstrated by the infamous writers' strike of 2007. I love this because of the irony – communication problems between communicators. The WGA (Writers Guild of America) and their producers, the AMPTP (Alliance of Motion Pictures and Television Producers), had three months of bitter negotiations over contracts. The long and short of the outcome was that they believed the key reason for the problem was a lack of communication from the start, which deepened the tension and distrust between the two parties. It wasn't until they met in small groups, well in to the negotiation, and got to know each other better that their talks "warmed up" and started to be productive. In the end they felt that if they had met more often to discuss concerns and goals the negotiation might not have had to happen.

Sometimes our knee-jerk response to what we think is negotiation is to start "giving in" or "giving away". Sometimes a client or a friend who is unhappy or confused makes a fuss about it. In order to keep peace and to smooth the road ahead, we may give up something. We can sometimes lose touch with the direction of a discussion, or confuse an objection with a signal to start negotiating.

So, we have hype about negotiation (we do it all the time about everything); stress (the other person might get the best of me, I'll lose control, I'll be taken advantage of or embarrassed); and varying levels of negotiation skill (learned from my dad, this-is-the-way-we-have always-done-it, a favorite book, did a workshop).

Most definitely we are spending a lot of high-powered time not understanding each other. Before you start, have the courage to clarify what is going on and what might be the next best step.

A changing attitude to negotiation

My inspiration for writing this book came about from years of working with students and with a range of clients across different industries on high-stakes negotiations. A particular joy for me is that what works well for negotiators in a boardroom, or between a major company and its acquirer, is fundamentally the same as for a salary negotiation, community or non-profit negotiation, and even negotiating with your partner or your kids.

It's likely that if you are good at negotiating a deal on used furniture you have a great start at what it takes to be good at buying or selling companies. Many of the skills for negotiating success in the boardroom are the same as negotiating success at the flea-market – and the people who do well at negotiating come in all shapes and sizes, personalities and skill levels.

I am noticing a change in temperament towards negotiating. My clients and students talk of being tired of gearing up to "compete" with others with whom they share interests, or fed up with "playing the negotiating game", "cracking the code", dealing with traps, tactics, and guessing games.

Many clients, some accustomed to complex negotiations with legacy obstacles and processes, often with many different groups and interests involved, some taking years or decades to settle, are opting to do something different from what they have always done.

One client has shifted from years of "cards held tightly to the chest – show me yours, I'll show you mine" – to more open discussions involving the opposing teams at the start of negotiation. The two parties agree on ground rules, objectives, and even get to know each other more personally before any official negotiation starts.

Another client has thrown out his old practice of preparing for negotiation in "opposite corners" and instead proposes his version of an "open house" so both parties can check assumptions and answer questions face to face.

Another has introduced what they call "pre-play" meetings where they brainstorm the question "What would it look like if we didn't need to negotiate?" This enables them to explore possibilities and has led to creative ideas that streamline processes and often obviates the need for the sort of negotiation they have always done.

Another re-negotiates contracts with suppliers every year by inviting them in to an open planning session to discuss needs and priorities for the following year.

In my classes I am now using a role-play simulation that sets up students to negotiate with full information on both sides at the start. This not only surprises them, it delights them too. The solutions they create in the time available are extraordinary.

Certainly everything is not love, peace, and unicorns. These approaches require taking a chance on trusting that the other side will work the same way. It doesn't work all the time, but it works most of the time.

This temperamental change, along with demands put on us from our changing world, lends promise to usher in an environment that favors a more "Nimble" style of negotiation.

So, what does it take to be a Nimble Negotiator?

Nimble Negotiating is an approach that embraces both ancient and conventional wisdom, with a modern twist. The twist recognizes that the way negotiation works is more like a basket-weave than a ball of string. It's a blending of many skills to be used when you need them and not if you don't, rather than a linear, step-by-step progression.

Nimbleness is a mindset that allows you to do what you need to do in the moment. It gives you the courage to have a plan, to interrogate, clarify, and be ready and willing to do something completely different. Leave your ego at the door.

What I think of as Nimble Negotiating requires three key skills:

- *The Nimble mindset:* this means you are mentally, physically, and emotionally prepared to make the best of what unfolds in front of you during a negotiation. I like to call it "disciplined compassion" at work. By compassion I mean responding to others in the context of the negotiation in a way that reflects an understanding of and interest in their needs. This is not making it up as you go along, rather being open to *learning* as you go along and making conscious adjustments in the moment.

- *Preparation:* when clarity is your objective, preparation takes on a new rigor and precision. There is too much information available, so you have to be selective about what is relevant and what isn't. Tip: there is a premium on insight. Nimble Negotiators opt for as much insight as possible gathered first-hand from their negotiating partners. The best negotiators are always the most prepared and nothing will ever take the place of preparation as the greatest of all game changers.

- *Communication:* some of the world's best ideas and best-laid plans end up in the trash can because they are badly communicated. A Nimble Negotiator needs a range of finely tuned communication skills in order to be flexible. Key skills are listening, and being able to confront, ask great questions, answer great questions, explain things clearly, convince, compel, persuade.

All of these key skills will be addressed in this book.

The importance of reconnaissance

Being a Nimble Negotiator means you know the lay of the land before you start negotiating. Yes, it matters.

My grandfather was a trench runner in France during World War I. Runners were the men who were primarily responsible for passing messages on foot from one command to another, often doing critical reconnaissance so that troops could move accurately and safely between posts. It was dangerous work and required speed and accuracy as you maneuvered in and out of trenches, often under cover of darkness and under enemy fire.

My grandfather explained that reconnaissance was one of the most important aspects of his job. This included revealing the location of the enemy and intelligence-gathering, which often resulted in decisions that meant shorter skirmishes and fewer casualties. Setting out on a reconnaissance duty was always fraught with danger but, when the runner made it back, his discoveries gave the decision-makers critical insight before any action was taken.

I believe reconnaissance principles like this also apply to negotiation. The better we manage and cope with the built-in uncertainty and unpredictability of negotiation, the more effective we will be. Just like the noble trench runner, what you learn about the landscape determines your best next move.

A Nimble approach can allow you to cut the time it takes to reach agreement, reduce tension, and improve your outcomes. Success with this approach relies on your physical, emotional, and mental willingness to seek clarity first, then if need be to let go of your plans, sometimes a little, sometimes a lot. This requires good preparation and an open mind.

You may already be on your way to being a Nimble Negotiator. If so, well done on being part of the revolution! I want this book to give you confidence that you can replace stale habits and old ways of approaching negotiation.

Communication in order to reach agreement over who gets what is part of navigating everyday life. The rest of this book focuses on the key skills and techniques you need to make it a pleasure.

two

Going with the Flow

A man will be imprisoned
in a room with a door that's unlocked and opens inwards;
as long as it does not occur to him to pull rather than push.
Ludwig Wittgenstein

In most Western-style negotiation there is a range of cultural protocols about how much information (a lot or a little) is given out beforehand, and about when and how negotiations take place; there are strict guidelines about structure, behavior, and content that affect the shape of the negotiation process. All of this brings an order or sequence: a recognizable beginning, middle, and end. In theory, the process is expected to be judicious, linear, rational, and efficient. In practice, the in-the-room ethos is mostly competitive, assertive, urgent, and opaque.

Nimble Negotiating is a response to the "fatigue" associated with order or prescribed arrangement in the approach to negotiating. I mentioned in Chapter One that the skills you need to succeed as a negotiator today are formed more like a basket-weave (you need to be able to pull from a range of skills that are woven together – when you need them) rather than a line or a piece of string (e.g. "I always take control of the meeting early and always make them give the first offer").

As a Nimble Negotiator you have a well-prepared plan, yet you go with the flow.

Anything can happen.

Here's how to go with the flow.

Clarify

One of the main failings of the negotiator who isn't properly prepared is: *you may know what you can give, but not what you can get.*

A lot of negotiating suffers from the endemic problem that most people are not sure how to set a clear objective. By objective I mean an answer to the question "What do I expect as an overall outcome?" or "What do I want the other person to do or think?" A good way to get to an objective is to imagine that at the end of the negotiation someone asks you, "How did it go?" Assuming it had gone well, your answer could be something like "We got what we wanted on three critical issues" or "The client renewed the contract with our two most important criteria secured" or "We got the price we wanted for the house and the closing date suits our moving plans." Having a clear objective means you and/or your team are aligned with what you want to achieve and what you think is possible; you also have a shared and understood starting point. A coordinate against which to measure progress and success.

By clarifying an objective at the start of a negotiation, you are better able to determine if negotiation is your best next step. You'll find if you are honest about your objective, it means you have checked, clarified, and confirmed with the other party/person before you begin. This up-front action sets the stage for whatever happens next.

You may discover that it's not appropriate or opportune to negotiate. Maybe you or they aren't ready. Best to know before you start.

What if we aren't negotiating?

As a Nimble Negotiator, you might decide that the situation requires another of your persuasive skills, such as presenting, pitching, confronting, selling, probing, listening, having a strategic or learning conversation. For example:

- A manager prepares for a salary negotiation with her boss only to find that, instead, she first needs to make a clearer and more relevant case for how she would improve the individual performance of some of her team members.

- A salesperson doesn't realize he is expected to negotiate and ends up in a slightly confusing, aggressive, or embarrassing discussion with a client.
- A parent enters into an argument with their teenager about house rules and conduct that ends in both retreating to separate rooms.
- A team preparing for an annual fee negotiation with an existing client realizes that the meeting is instead about the client sending the business out to tender.
- An entrepreneur prepares thoroughly for a meeting to negotiate financing with a likely investor and learns in the meeting that the investor is more curious about the business than interested in investing at the moment.

Other situations where you are not negotiating but instead presenting, pitching, or investigating include:

- A meeting or presentation where you make a proposal that recommends a specific course of action.
- Proposing a fee increase to a client.
- Suggesting a particular holiday destination to your partner.
- Presenting results of your research.
- Delivering bad or good news.
- Deciding what the family should have for breakfast.
- Presenting changes or next steps to your colleagues or clients.
- Handling an objection, conflict, or disagreement.
- Discussing with your child's teacher what activities you will volunteer for on parents' day.
- Arguing with your child about whether or not they will wear a raincoat.
- Getting a refund on merchandise at a store.
- Presenting a new idea.

Persuading and influencing are certainly skills required to be a good negotiator, but that doesn't mean that every occasion requiring persuasion or influence is a negotiation. Think about negotiating as being identified by the act of exchanging, trading, apportioning value. In any of the cases listed above, your pitching, presenting, listening, or other skills may be more appropriate.

OK, now we *are* negotiating

On the other hand, having considered your objective, you may discover that it is exactly right and that negotiating is what you should be doing. A Nimble Negotiator recognizes and prepares for the sequence (order or flow) I mentioned at the start of this chapter and understands that Nimbleness trumps sequence.

Because even with the best laid plans for your negotiation, surprises are guaranteed. Any number of twists and turns, unexpected people, issues, behavior good and bad, may pop up to remind you that this is real life.

Let me give you a couple of examples to illustrate this classic linear concept of sequencing/flow in negotiation. My client Michael had to negotiate with a school board for the installation of new solar panels. My friend Susan wanted to negotiate with her boss about a change to her work schedule. What follows are the ideal negotiation steps, in their ideal order. Each step has a name and a function. You may be doing something similar already.

Step One: Pre-negotiation tactics

These are behaviors designed to manipulate expectations about how things are going to turn out, or create awareness before a negotiation even begins. I have seen these tactics range from the elaborate to the sublime! They are used to manage how the other side feels about the outcome before you even "get in the room".

In Michael's case, he learned that, before he could begin the negotiation, it was in the interests of both sides that he create a better understanding about solar as an energy solution (each of the board members had doubts, but for different reasons based on different experiences). One month before their meeting, Michael organized an article/interview feature in the local paper about the benefits of solar; he collected testimonials from the principals of other schools that were using solar and sent them to the board members; and he had individual discussions with each board member about market data and financial comparisons. His goal was to give everyone a better understanding of the concept of solar and help them feel more comfortable with it; he hoped having individual conversations would clear the air.

Susan's commute was a total of four hours a day and she wanted to spend a day each week working from home. It was widely known that her boss was not comfortable with the idea of telecommuting. Susan's plan was to drip-feed (as she called it) positive information and experiences to him before she approached him with the request. This drip-feed included ensuring they had a friendly "run into each other" in the hallways and at the coffee machine so he could see that she arrived early and worked late; during one of the regular team meetings she made an informal presentation about trends in work-life balance, which led to an open and interesting group discussion.

How you behave toward your negotiating partners always matters. How you behave toward them at the beginning of a negotiation has a powerful effect on the outcome and the ease with which you move through it. Tread carefully.

Step Two: Opening

The opening is an opportunity to set the tone or mood right up front and to establish goals, parameters, and expectations, so you are ready to talk. Ideally you have a face-to-face meeting but in some cases there could be an initial phone call and/or email as well. The opening is best done conversation-style and is intended to establish mutual purpose, set an objective and an agenda, and gain agreement on rules and procedures.

One of the most important things a Nimble Negotiator can do at this stage is to demonstrate an understanding of the other party's position. Make it your goal to clarify by probing and listening. This will help shed light on issues for both sides. If you probe for real issues early on, you will save time later. No wasting time on things you already agree about or on minor issues.

A good example of "ground rules" for your opening could include:

- Nothing is agreed until everything is agreed.
- No subject is closed until everyone agrees it should be closed.
- New issues or material may be introduced at any time before the finish of the negotiation.

- Clarity is essential. If you don't understand something, ask (always useful, but absolutely critical for cross-cultural or phone meetings).

Include whatever else you can think of that is relevant to your meeting.

Procedural details play an important role in clearing everyone's minds of distractions about logistics and roles, etc. Here are some examples of opening remarks:

- Acknowledge that everyone is present and indicate the start of the meeting.
- Welcome and introduce people as required.
- Indicate the purpose of the meeting and what you hope to achieve.
- State the time schedule, including breaks and meals.
- Mention any other pertinent procedural details.
- Handle any preliminary questions.

Michael also spent a little time up front asking if there were any questions and thanking everyone for assisting him in his insight-gathering over the past few weeks. This acknowledged support he had already received and drew attention to his own extra-thorough effort.

Susan's arrangements were, of course, less formal than this. She sent her boss an email asking to discuss a work-life balance idea she had for herself and fixed a meeting for the following week.

Step Three: Initial probing and discussion

This step involves some exploration, asking questions to find common ground, uncovering obstacles, discussions, information, possible sticking points, key issues or concerns. There's no give and take happening yet.

Michael knew from his homework that a couple of the board members didn't believe the school had money in the budget for solar panels, and others thought the money was there but the timing was wrong. He needed to expose these "elephants in the room" and let the individuals openly discuss their concerns.

Susan put her proposal to her boss and listened to his counter-arguments. By probing them and seeking greater understanding of the obstacles, she learned that he had two core objections: "I think the team need to be together rather than on their own or isolated" and "I am not convinced people are productive at home."

Initial probing and discussion will help you lay the groundwork for exploring more deeply as you go along.

Step Four: Re-strategize

After some possible new discoveries/learning, go away if necessary or re-strategize on the spot and then re-group.

Michael's board met on a monthly basis, so rather than re-strategize before the next formal session he planned a number of informal one-on-one meetings with specific members, to clarify, enlighten, or answer any queries. He'd learned a lot in his preparations over the past weeks but now he had an opportunity to keep the momentum going with a few individuals.

After her initial discussions Susan needed to go away and gather some more specific information about company policy, competitor human resource policy, best practices, and productivity data. She and her boss scheduled another meeting for a week later.

Step Five: Initial proposals

It is time to test the water and begin to get the feel for the scope of the give and take.

It is important that you decide what your initial proposal or "opening position" is, well in advance of your meeting. We'll discuss the intricacies of preparing this opening position in Chapter Six. For the moment, keep in mind that you don't want to be so tough or unreasonable that you create bad feeling (always hard to claw back), or so ill-informed that you do an easy deal and suffer from wondering if you did as well as you could have (aka winner's curse).

Your opening needs to show you have done some homework and are close enough to the other party's offer, as you understand it, to show a real possibility of agreement and yet still leave room to maneuver.

When you state your positions and issues up front, do it in a courteous and respectful tone as if you expect to have these issues and positions tested and modified. Don't set yourself up for a protracted struggle by sounding too confident or determined to get your way.

Traditionally, the party who is seeking the money or the benefit to be derived from the negotiation makes the first proposal. For example, the seller of the house, the vendor, Michael, Susan. Not always, but usually. As a rule of thumb, it's best to go first. Much more on that in Chapter Six.

When the initial positions are presented, be calm, restate them, explore, and probe. You can consider resolving one issue at a time or put all the issues out at once and discuss priorities. Either way, you have an opportunity to set the tone of an intelligent, respectful, non-game playing, and Nimble negotiator.

Michael decided to focus on what he knew were the most important issues right up front. So in his initial proposal he targeted overall cost, timing of the cash outlay, and return on investment.

At Susan's second meeting she made an initial proposal to work from home one day per week.

Step Six: Initial concession trading

Explore more deeply what you've learned after you've both made your initial proposals. Find out the reasons behind the proposals, test what the other side is actually prepared to give/trade at this point, and explore any alternatives that may be possible. Narrow down to the real issues. The real skill in concession trading is being able to look at all the issues and then, using your position on one of them, gain a concession from the other party on a separate issue.

Two more types of concession trading to keep in mind while we are at it: issue trading and process trading. Simply put, *issue* trading involves giving or getting a concession on something that has value to one or both of you.

Process trading involves trading an intangible that is related to the *process* of the negotiation rather than any issue. Say, I concede on a different start time or place for the meeting or I agree to a one-on-one meeting first without the rest of the team.

Process trading is a clever way to create obligation or debt because, in effect, I have conceded something that is outside the area of our negotiation and not desperately important (to me, at least). This usually means I'll be able to get a concession on something that does matter – an issue!

Back to Michael. He learned more about the obstacles he faced and the board members' priorities. It emerged that one of the main concerns over the timing of the cash outlay was how it would affect an existing commitment to buy new lights to illuminate the school baseball field for night games. Michael had some wiggle room on both the overall cost of materials and the timing for construction. He was therefore able to lower the price (bargaining) and propose a different billing cycle (out of a facilities budget) that would enable the board to pay for the installation of the panels after they had installed the baseball field lighting (concession trading).

Susan's boss accepted her proposal to telecommute one day per week, but on a trial basis. She agreed to a morning and afternoon catch-up meeting (which they would have via Skype) to discuss the day's output. In three months they would re-evaluate. He asked that in return for working at home, she do some additional administrative tasks that didn't require interaction with others. He also proposed she telecommute on Tuesday or Wednesday so she could be present for team meetings Monday morning.

Step Seven: Final trading

At this point, usually final trading can take place. It is a good time to probe for anything else and check for levels of commitment.

Michael came up with a way to allow the board to fulfill their commitment to the baseball team by altering the cash flow requirements. There were trade-offs made with the number of panels (they were increased) and the cost (reduced); the lighting of the baseball field (with solar compatibility) could be completed before the next season.

Susan agreed to use the three-month trial as an opportunity to shape some guidelines, rules, and best practices for telecommuting in the future. She and her boss agreed to put a time-cap on the extra administrative duties. Susan agreed to a Wednesday telecommute day.

Step Eight: Closing

Time to restate and acknowledge everything that has been agreed and to create next steps. Be sure that you understand all the agreements and concessions and that you have heard the other party say them back to you. Listen carefully. Review your notes.

Closing remarks can include:

- Summarizing briefly what took place and what was achieved.
- Re-stating important conclusions or agreements.
- Establishing if there are any next steps, meetings, things that need to be done and, if so, stating by whom and by when they are to be completed.
- Thanking everyone for their time, attention, and any particular contribution they've made.
- Stating that the meeting is over.

Chapter Nine focuses specifically on closing, so if you'd like more detail, have a visit there.

Michael and the board agreed on a contract completion date and an estimated start time for the solar project. Michael noted a need to follow up with one member who was still confused about his discounted cash flow calculations and with many of the others who had requested further information or expressed interest in various aspects of the work.

Susan and her boss exchanged Skype addresses and agreed on the timings and agenda for their daily check-in. Agreements were reiterated. Next steps were for Susan and her boss to announce the plans to her co-workers at the next available Monday team meeting.

Step Nine: Delivery/Maintenance

Do what you said you were going to do and deliver on expectations (or better!).

Back in the real world

So, there's an x-ray of the bones of a classic flow of Western-style negotiation. Wouldn't it be great if everything worked as orderly as this?

As I mentioned, the reality of the flow of any negotiation is that, despite your excellent preparation, anything can happen. People are often not well prepared or have a different understanding of what the outcome should be. Emotion can take over – people compete, individuals disagree or argue over issues they are trying to "win" or "not lose". Surprises abound: grandstanding, shyness, pride, fear, greed, lust, nepotism, love, hate, exaggeration, lying, you name it. Hopefully not all at once.

Here's what Michael actually discovered:

- At the very start of the negotiation he was told solar was too expensive and tax-inefficient for a public entity.
- There was no money allocated in the budget for solar or any capital expenditure this year.
- One board member had a cousin who was trying to convince the board to consider geo-thermal.
- Three weeks into the negotiation one key supporting board member resigned due to illness.

Susan discovered that her boss was intending to offer her a promotion that meant she would be working at another office even further away from home.

All part of life's rich tapestry, and all in a day's work for a Nimble Negotiator.

The importance of preparation

Even though they hadn't foreseen these outcomes, Michael and Susan had both brought thorough planning to their negotiations. I'll show you more about that in the next chapter. They understood their preferences and constraints very well – what they could and couldn't give – and, as important, understood what the other person/party valued and could or was likely to give in return.

Nimble Negotiators tend to spend 30% more time up front, exploring, learning, asking, and clarifying, often face to face with the other party/person. Alternatives and creative possibilities are often uncovered. This helps set clearer and often agreed-upon objectives and lays the groundwork for the rest of the negotiation.

When the flow doesn't go smoothly

When confronted with an obstacle or an objection during the negotiation, the Nimble Negotiator tests it and understands it before responding.

The quality of relationships between people in the negotiation factors highly into the Nimble Negotiator's overall objectives.

What about flow if you run into someone who doesn't play nice? More on that in Chapter Four: Managing Tension. Nimble mantra: Don't panic. You always have a choice about whether or not to continue. You don't have to take abuse. Really.

Every negotiation has a flow of some kind as the negotiators work together toward an agreement. The flow is not likely to be what you expect, but there will be one. The sequence of events may be different or you may skip steps entirely. The key to going with the flow is staying aware of what is happening and adjusting accordingly.

Sometimes you have to go where you're not expecting. Consider it the fun part.

three

The Nimble Planning Path

It does not do to leave a live dragon out of your cal-
culations, if you live near him.
J.R.R. *Tolkien*

A well-conceived plan sharpens objectives, exposes possible obstacles, and highlights alternatives and new ideas. Even though you may not know exactly how it will all come out until you are actually negotiating, it is still important to have a plan. As Antonio Machado said, "Wanderer, there is no road. The road is made by walking."

Another important factor that defines your approach to negotiation is your attitude towards it. A critical question to ask (and remind) yourself or your team is "What do we want our relationship to be with this person or this group after we finish the negotiation?" It's important because, once you decide, it will affect every aspect of your planning as well as the way you behave and communicate. For example, how effective is it to negotiate with someone who has said they want to work cooperatively with you and then behave badly and watch the negotiation crumble due to trust breaking down?

Your actions define your character. Make your actions consistent with your attitude.

With that spirit in mind, let's begin to plan.

Step One: Reconnaissance

You recall my example of the WWI trench runners from Chapter One and the power of getting the lay of the land before taking action in a negotiation? One of the biggest differences between a Nimble Negotiator and everyone else is the gathering and harnessing of the first-hand information and insight you need from the people with whom you are negotiating. Your intention is to create the most value from your negotiation for everyone involved. This includes communicating directly with whoever you are negotiating with (or intend to negotiate with) early in the planning process and continuing to ask and clarify when you need to throughout the negotiation. This kind of active engagement with the "other side" is a bit of an anathema in most negotiations. Many people approach negotiation like a game, seeking to gain advantage for their side by out-smarting, out-manipulating, and generally using competitive tactics in order to win. They become experts on their own deal but neglect the importance of understanding the other side. While even the Nimblest negotiator needs to understand their own position (as a minimum!), you will make the biggest positive difference by reaching out to the other party, early.

Recently I was approached by one of my students about her upcoming salary negotiation. She had the overall goal of asking for an increase and had established some facts about her own performance, what others were being paid for a similar role in her industry, and what salary she wanted in order to be satisfied in the job going forward.

I learned that she was not sure of when or how to have the conversation with her boss. She said he was an awkward person and generally uncomfortable with this type of conversation. There was no set procedure in place that she knew of.

We decided she should do some reconnaissance – check out the situation before taking action. Instead of marching into her boss's office with a negotiation in mind, perhaps starting with a restatement of the highlights of her stellar performance review and then announcing her opening position or objective, she would first have a conversation with him, learn a little more about his experience and how he understood the process worked.

Mary set up an informal meeting in Brian's office. The conversation went something like this:

Mary: "Thanks for making time, Brian. I am interested in exploring a couple of things with you. I'd like to understand a little about how our company process works for salary review conversations. Then, about how I go about organizing a salary review conversation for myself."

Brian (laughs uncomfortably): "So, are you looking for a salary increase? Things are pretty tight now with HQ, I doubt they'd even entertain the question."

Mary: "I'm considering it. At the moment, I am interested in the review process. I thought you could shed some light on how it works."

Brian (speaking quickly, a little nervously): "Well, you know, it's different for different people. We have been growing so fast it's hard to keep up with the new hires and changes going on in all the divisions. Jobs are hard to come by, so I think everyone is grateful to be working. I don't think there have been many salary increases."

Mary: "Have you personally been involved in any conversations about salary reviews that gave you some insight about how the process would work for me?"

And so on. Mary focused her questions on learning what Brian knew about the salary review process. She remained calm and friendly, and didn't get drawn into making the conversation about her own salary review.

She learned he was not the person with whom she needed to focus her negotiation planning, though he was certainly an influencer and had a vote. She learned there was an ideal time of year to discuss reviews, and that a panel of specific senior managers made the final decision. She also learned, as an incidental to the discussion, that the company was growing rapidly in another division and having a hard time filling positions.

Hearing this completely changed her planning and approach. In her effort to clarify, she found opportunity. Instead of just asking for a rise in her current job, she discovered she was eligible for an exciting opportunity in another division. She also learned her salary review was not a negotiation she was supposed to have with her boss.

Don't be frightened of clarity

In my experience, openness, desire for clarity, and intention to be fair will disarm some and encourage others. There is no evidence to suggest that if you are open in negotiations you will suffer exploitation. A recent study conducted by Leigh Thompson from the Kellogg School of Management showed that negotiators who provide information to the other party about their interests improve their outcome, or profits, by over 10%. Also, if one negotiator reveals insights or interests, the likelihood is double that the other side will reveal theirs. This is called the reciprocity principle. In studies on reciprocity, under normal conditions, the incidence of providing information to the other party is 19%. But when negotiators provide information to the people they are negotiating with, it jumps to 40%.

I have found a similar result in my classes as well as my client negotiation consulting. Approaching a negotiation prepared to reveal and fine-tuning your ability to "see" the reveal signals from the other side are powerful skills.

Good negotiation preparation involves making sound decisions based on fact and insight, not just speculation and guessing. Often too much planning takes place in opposite corners, with everyone absorbed in private preparation. Nimble Negotiators focus early planning on asking and clarifying so they can:

- Determine if a negotiation is indeed the right next step for the situation (as opposed to some other type of persuasive communication – look back at Chapter One for possible alternatives). Often it can be as simple as the need to handle an objection, clarify a misunderstanding, persuasively pitch an idea, or probe more deeply for understanding.
- Cut the time needed for negotiating overall by uncovering priorities, opportunities, obstacles, and areas of concern. You will get the added bonus of building rapport with this approach.

At the beginning this means that before any negotiating objectives, proposals, positions, trades, or concessions are even considered, there is ideally face-to-face, first-hand exchange of insight and information. This is a conversation that doesn't attempt to negotiate.

Seeking to clarify early can be off-putting to some. If they respond by refusing or are reluctant to participate, this can be revealing about their expectations and principles.

I encourage you to step up and see how a reconnaissance conversation can set the tone for your negotiations. I have used this technique myself and coached others enough to know it generates important insights and reaps interesting rewards most of the time.

Venture outside your comfort zone.

More reconnaissance

So, have I made the case for you to do better reconnaissance? Hope so. Let's get back to Step One on the Planning Path.

Here are two sample lists of reconnaissance questions that may be useful for you to choose from.

The first list is to help you determine/diagnose if you need/want to/can/should negotiate, or what type of interaction you may be better off having.

The second list is all the other questions that may guide you towards a better understanding of your negotiating partners and crafting the best outcomes.

Pick and choose from these lists and refine as needed. They are not in any particular order.

List One: Are we negotiating?
- Tell me a little about your expectations for our meeting.
- I'm interested in learning more about….
- Would you clarify something/a few issues for me?
- What brings you here?
- In an ideal world, what would you like to achieve?
- What else would you like to achieve?
- How would you characterize the issue/problem?
- What is most important to you?
- Why is that most important?
- What is least important to you?

- What would be a good outcome for you?
- What's blocking you?
- What do you fear might happen if we don't solve this?
- How is this a problem/issue for you?
- How do you think this is a problem for others?
- How can I help you avoid any harm?
- If the problem were solved, what would be different?
- How would the change you are talking about make a difference for you?
- How do you see our relationship evolving if we solve this problem?
- What do you think is fair?
- Why do you think that's fair?
- How can I be of service to you?
- Is there anything we shouldn't do or say?
- What would the outcome of this discussion/our negotiation be if you were to walk out the door thinking it was good for you?

List Two: Preparing for your negotiation
<u>*The person*</u>
- What is their negotiation style? Do they have a reputation for being aggressive and direct, or are they reserved and quiet?
- What is their work background, social background, education level?
- What is their negotiating experience? Sales, procurement, contracts, mediation, arbitration, etc?
- How much do you know about what they do? About their business?
- Are there any local customs or prejudices to be aware of?
- What issues outside the negotiation are important to them right now?
- What do they want?
- What do they need?
- Whose opinion do they respect?
- What are they proud of or loyal to?
- What excites them?
- What ideas, experiences, or feelings do you have in common?

Your negotiation

- How much do they know about you? About why you are negotiating? What is their attitude towards you?
- What are they expecting from you – an initial or exploratory discussion? Completing the negotiation in one meeting?
- Is timing important?
- How might the negotiation be jeopardized as a result of this issue/problem?
- What should you not say?
- How do they make decisions? What process/steps do they follow? What criteria will they use to make decisions?
- Will you be negotiating with the person who has authority to make decisions?
- What questions will you ask?
- What questions will they ask? What do you hope they don't ask? What are your answers and (if relevant) which member of your team will answer?
- What else might influence the decision?
- Can they act now? Are there obstacles to overcome before they can accept your offers? Are there obstacles to closing the deal?

Step Two: Based on what you have learned, decide on the subject and plan your negotiation objective

It is important to have a clear subject and objective as it provides discipline and focus during planning. Your subject is defined as the actual "about what" of your negotiation. In other words, are you resolving a disagreement or conflict, pursuing a partnership, building a working relationship, or just haggling? Note: You must have your objective clear for yourself. Simple example: "Buying a car" is not an objective as such. "Buying the best low-mileage car that I can with my $10,000 budget" is an objective. It can't be so broad as to be meaningless.

As I explained in Chapter Two, your objective should be a broad statement of what you expect as an overall outcome. Keep in mind that the importance of having an objective needs to be balanced by your willingness to be open to the unexpected and to any obstacles that might cause you to revise or re-think your approach.

If you are unable to gain agreement about an objective with the other party/person during planning, that's okay. It's not always possible. You will discover infinitely more during the negotiation.

Step Three: Identify the issues and interests for you and the other party

An issue is best described as something that has value to one or both parties and can be "traded". If it can't be traded as such, it can be a factor that affects the perception of the value of what you have to offer.

One of the most common mistakes is to treat every issue equally. This can lead to a huge time-waster because people spend equal time preparing insight on the important as on the less important. I was involved in a negotiation between a Nature Conservancy and a developer over the developer's proposal to build a retail and housing complex in a pristine wilderness. In simple terms, the Conservancy's key issue was protecting the local watershed (river), but they also put forward a host of other issues as negotiating ploys. The developers treated all these issues as equally important. After two years with no progress they finally realized that the Conservancy valued watershed protection above everything, but not necessarily to the exclusion of all development. It can take sometimes take several discussions to get this out in more complex negotiation.

As early as possible in your planning, you need to ask or clarify, "What are the issues that are important to you?" and, in particular, which ones are critical. Find out if there are any showstoppers – those issues that if they can't be agreed would cause a negotiation breakdown. You may also find new issues that you didn't expect. Time spent in the planning stage on understanding what the other party cares about and what they believe they can "trade" is time well spent.

Here is a checklist to use as a guide:

- What are the real issues?
- How flexible/inflexible are you on these issues?
- What is of value and how should it be apportioned?
- Do you and your team members agree that these are the real issues to be negotiated?
- What is your true position on the issues?

- What is the other party's position on the issues?
- Did you learn this first-hand or is it your assumption?
- How far apart to you seem to be before the negotiations start?
- What are the break issues (the issues that may cause the negotiation to break down if they are not agreed upon)?

Step Four: Identify strengths and weaknesses for issues on both sides

This can take a bit of time but is worth it. It can be critical to get a better understanding of the relative strength and weakness of issues for both sides. For those issues where you are strong, you can take a harder position, but you must be practical and acknowledge your own weaknesses too.

A good example is the man who was selling his property in Napa Valley. He had spent 15 years lovingly growing heritage apples, only to find that all prospective buyers saw the land as only suitable for vineyards. It would take years to turn the apple orchard into a productive grape crop. In the end, he sold his land for less than its intrinsic value, to reflect the cost to a purchaser of having to remove the trees to put in vines.

Sad. What he had viewed as a strength (a mature apple orchard) was viewed by the purchasers as a weakness. Taking the time to identify strengths and weaknesses will shed light on the reality of your situation. Sometimes new opportunities and issues will appear. You may learn that you need solid answers and explanations for questions that hadn't occurred to you before, and you will learn questions you need or want to ask. Mostly, you gain perspective, so do it.

Step Five: Decide your approach (aka strategy) for each issue

Your approach needs to be consistent with your overall attitude to the negotiation. If you decide at the start of your planning that you want to preserve the relationship with the other person and work towards fairness to everyone involved, then you won't choose an approach that would risk any of that. I'm surprised how often individuals who say they value the relationship with their counterparty yet enter the room like a gorilla.

If you start by assigning an approach to each issue individually you are also less likely inadvertently to bundle or mash issues together, only to discover later that you have given something away that you didn't mean to, or have not dealt thoroughly with something important to you. For example, with issues that you know are important to you personally or professionally, you might consider being more cautious and a little less quick to compromise. For things that are less important you may feel you can be flexible early and easily. Here are some approaches that are commonly used:

- *High-trust* means you are prepared to "put all your cards on the table" and be direct and transparent with the other person. While it may help get to the point quicker, with the wrong person your openness could be used against you. In a high-trust approach, for example, you might include your company's background financial data on costs to support the issue of a price increase, but if you do this with the wrong person you could find them leaking this confidential information or using it to gain leverage with your competitors.
- *Tough-tough* is when you decide you won't reveal much about where you stand on an issue and compromises won't be easy. This can backfire by damaging the relationship or making it hard to reach an agreement. Tough-tough is a "take-it-or-leave-it" approach. Options are not a consideration.
- *Tough-but-fair* means you have done your homework very well. You understand enough about the situation to make an offer that is fair to both sides and you don't budge from it. You know it is fair and they know it is fair. The act of not budging makes it tough. The knowledge of equity makes it fair. For example, a lawyer friend specializing in commercial real estate has an established reputation for knowing her offers are fair and sticking to her guns. In her industry, while there are a lot of individual idiosyncrasies about buildings, the market practices, prices, terms, etc are widely known. The catch is you need to know enough about the other party's position and their situation to recognize if any facts they present are being manipulated. As

the saying goes, "Everyone is entitled to their own opinion, but not to their own facts."

- *Flexible*: this approach shows that you are fair and reasonable and prepared to be flexible. The downside is that you can be seen as indecisive or a pushover.
- *Yielding*: this is where you are prepared to give the others what they want on an issue, usually under pressure.

Step Six: Create your bargaining position for each issue

Here's where a piece of paper and a pencil come in handy. For each issue, draw a horizontal line across a page and on the left side of the line write your Best Possible opening position. This position is rarely agreed to in traditional negotiation, but you have to start somewhere. On the right side of the line, write your Worst Possible outcome.

Create two more positions in between. Repeat this for each issue and then think about what the other person/party might do in reverse. Their Best Possible opening position will line up with your Worst Possible, etc. In the middle you have the common ground or likely area of settlement.

Now it's time to test whether these positions match your overall attitude. I've seen many people say they can be flexible on a less important issue, only to put a really tough opening position on the left-hand side of the line. If your strategy on this issue is to be flexible, make sure your position reflects it.

A Nimble Negotiator will initiate a conversation and check to clarify the other person/party's position on an issue. Share your vague position and see how it lands. Just because you share it doesn't mean you have to agree to it. For example, "John, I'm not sure exactly how to evaluate this. Is it possible to be a bit more specific about what criteria you've used to price the product?" You can always say, "Now that I know what you need, I'll think a bit more about our/my offer."

Other ways to express a need for clarification include, "I want to make sure I understand your perspective on this issue" or "I understand that you feel strongly about the project finish date and I am not sure why that is important. I want to be sure I understand your perspective on this."

There may be an opportunity also to clarify or seek their advice about what would persuade them to change their point of view. "Is there anything I can do or say to persuade you to think differently about that?" or "What would you do if you were in my shoes?"

Step Seven: Decide your tactics

I'll talk a lot more about tactics in Chapter Four. For now, understand that tactics are the behaviors and actions that bring your overall attitude about the negotiation to life. There is no point in saying you want to be open and fair if your tactics are mean or rude. Intentionally withholding information, refusing to say what you think, stalling unnecessarily, introducing new information at the last minute are all tactics that frustrate and annoy others.

Your excellent planning should mean that you become more aware of what tactics the other side may use, know how to neutralize them (that's in Chapter Four too), and, if you are part of a team, agree on what tactics will and will not be used.

Again, most importantly, be sure the tactics (behaviors) you choose are consistent with the attitude you plan to bring to the negotiation.

Step Eight: Develop questions, answers, key messages, and evidence to support your position

You will discover some gaps in your understanding of the other person's needs and priorities and will need to talk to them to fill the gaps. Before your next conversation with them, write down what questions you need to ask to help you fine-tune your negotiation plan. Think about the questions they will ask you, plan your answers, and think about what evidence you need to have on hand to support your answers. As good as it is, your word is not enough. You'll likely need some evidence to support your position and make them rethink theirs. More on this in Chapter Seven.

Step Nine: Decide on your alternatives

You'll have a lot more confidence if you go into the final stages of a negotiation having thought through some creative alternatives to your original plans, a solid plan B, and some worst-case scenarios. One obvious alternative is to do nothing – that's okay too. See Chapter Six on opening positions and how to consider alternatives.

Step Ten: Rehearse important messages and responses

Your planning path comes to life if you can rehearse some of the critical messages and points you want to make and your responses to possibly touchy subjects or objections. Rehearsal is a high-level listening skill. You will be more comfortable explaining or persuading on important points if you are not doing it for the first time in the negotiation. You will be so glad you rehearsed. There can be a lot of tension in a negotiation; rehearsing is the most powerful way to manage and even reduce it.

To sum up

These simple yet effective planning steps will help you or your team focus on what's important and the actions that need to be in place before you negotiate. The order of the steps seems to work best as I have them here, although you may complete some steps, learn something new and go back, amend, and continue.

Keep in mind that there will always be mismatches between what you expect and what unfolds in a negotiation. Don't make assumptions. When in doubt, ask. You will be more likely to take actions that reflect reality.

And when there simply isn't time...

So, what if you only have an hour or a taxi-ride in which to prepare? Here are a couple of planning approaches if you have to move fast.

Fast-track One : "Back of the napkin" planning
- List all the issues under consideration.
- Prioritize issues (rank-order or percentage).
- Brainstorm the alternatives (yours and theirs).
- Decide the best possible outcomes/terms for each issue.
- Decide the best possible alternatives for each issue (yours and theirs).
- Prepare your opening offers/positions.

Fast Track Two: "Back of the business card" planning
- Identify your key goals.
- Brainstorm your alternatives.
- Prepare your opening position.

four

Managing Tension

The fibers of all things have their tension and are
strained like the strings of an instrument.

Henry David Thoreau

One of the most important skills of a Nimble Negotiator is being able to manage tension. By tension I mean how you respond to/cope with the uncomfortable or unexpected stuff that can happen during a negotiation, that feeling of fear or anxiety or even excitement that springs from the unknown or the unexpected. Tension can come from many places and it is different for everyone. Sometimes it is a difficult or angry person who is behaving badly; another time someone makes an unexpected objection or threatens a deadlock. Any of these combined with even the anticipation of a negotiation can be a volatile cocktail.

Tension is a natural part of human relationships and of negotiating in particular. Negotiation has a word for the kind of behavior that is designed to raise and lower tension. Tactics! In this chapter we'll talk about those and how to handle them.

It is important to remember that tension is not necessarily either good nor bad. It doesn't need to have a negative effect on you. It only has a negative effect on you if you let it.

Conventional negotiating wisdom has come a long way to taking some of the sting out of game-playing and old-fashioned hardball-style negotiating. More enlightened negotiators come to the table with a more positive intention, focusing on interests rather than fixed positions, seeking objectivity and mutual gain.

As a Nimble Negotiator you will have lessened the potential for tension further by doing a good deal of reconnaissance. You reduce surprises and create understanding by having the courage to ask or clarify as you go along. The reality of negotiating is that it is fluid and dynamic. You can't always predict people's responses. The Nimble Negotiator, however, is ready for anything.

It's not about you

This is always a difficult challenge because most of us are so focused on "getting it right" that we are thrown off track by other people's negative opinions and attitudes. If this happens to you, you feel it in your body. Maybe your heart beats faster, your face gets flushed or your hands feel clammy. You might feel a rush of embarrassment or anger. "Why did they do that?"

One of the most important lessons I have learned is that no matter what anyone says or does to you, it's not about you. It's about them. Oh how many years of angst I could have avoided if I could just say this to my younger self now! As Miguel Ruiz says in his beautiful book *The Four Agreements,* "By taking things personally, you set yourself up to suffer for nothing."

If you take something personally, the most common response is to become defensive. Worse, you feel angry, hurt, upset, or distracted. Maybe you even feel like verbally "fighting back". The result is you stop listening. Most people can't hide the physical symptoms for very long if they are offended, embarrassed, angry, or unsettled by something. Your color changes, you may fidget, look away or down, breathe in deeply, sigh, have a changed expression – or all of the above! Why let this response get in the way of clear communication?

The best first response when things get tough is to stay calm and present. Wait before responding, because you don't understand anything yet – except, of course, that it's not personal. Be calm because it allows you precious time to gather your wits. You only need to be calm and focused for a short time and the right response will be revealed to you. If you let your monkey-brain and your adrenal glands mindlessly lead the way ("I'm offended, let's attack!"), it is very difficult to claw back.

I promise that if you can find just ten silent seconds during a difficult situation to remain neutral, keep breathing, and wait before responding, it could be the most profound improvement you make to your negotiating skills. I always ask clients preparing for a negotiation to tell me what they hope the other side doesn't bring up. This way, if it does come up, we have already thought about how to respond to it. It is always a good idea to rehearse anyway, but it's particularly useful in managing tension.

Remember the Nimble mantra – don't panic. Don't take it personally, keep listening and clarify.

Let's have a look at the three most common types of situation that create tension in negotiation and what to do about them. They are: handling objections and resistance; deadlocks; and, finally, tactics.

Tension Situation One: Handling objections and resistance

Objections are a welcome part of any negotiation. They give you a clue or a signal and are an invitation to engage with someone on something that is of concern to them. You are handed the opportunity to clear the air, explain, educate, or re-position an idea. Given the value they can possibly bring to the outcome of your negotiation, objections are worth handling well.

It's always important to remember that when a person is objecting or resisting something, there is a certain amount of tension building up from their point of view. Resistance or objection is physical and emotional for the other person because they are often fearful, surprised, angry, or confused.

Sometimes a valid objection is a valid objection. It's good practice to acknowledge it and handle it in the best way possible. Owning up works wonders for your credibility and relationship. More on that later in the chapter.

Here are some simple techniques that work for handling objections and resistance. Since Nimble Negotiators value clarity, let's start by clarifying the objection. Then, once you know what it is, handle it the appropriate way.

Clarify

If the question or objection is too vague or too general, ask them to be specific

Ask directly for the objection, for example, "Why do you feel it's unreasonable?" or "What is it you don't like about the proposal?"

Ask questions like:

- Would you explain that a little further?
- Would you elaborate a little on how the proposal might not be compatible with your expectations?
- What difficulties, specifically, do you think we will have if we go ahead with it?

If there is more than one objection, pinpoint the priorities

Find out which objection is most important. You'll find that the less important objections will take care of themselves when the more important ones are overcome. Also, once you find out the priorities, you won't waste time and energy mitigating less important issues.

Ask questions like:

- Of the three challenges you mentioned, which is the most problematical?
- Why is that?

If what they object to is partially valid, concede the obvious

Sometimes objections have some good points. It is a good idea to acknowledge this as part of your answer. Beware of the "but" trap, though. You hear it all the time. "I think your idea has merit, but... (insert rebuttal)." You may as well say, "I think your idea has merit, but you're an idiot."

Instead, remove the word but. You don't need it. Add a pause or an "and' or, if you must, a "however". "But" is an overused word that we use when we haven't bothered to craft our response in a more thoughtful way.

Try "You make a good point" or "The first point you make is valid and shows a good understanding of our resource requirements. Your second point is one with which I disagree."

Now that you understand the objection, it's time to handle it. Depending on what you discover or understand, here are some options:

Listen

To handle an objection well, you need to listen to it. Not just at the beginning, but all the way through. Often a person needs to know that you understand them before they can accept what you have to say. This means you resist the temptation to interrupt and you let people complete their thoughts and questions. Sometimes people just need to be listened to and the problem will air itself out.

Give needed information

The easiest and most successful way to handle an objection is to give the needed information or the answer in a way that eliminates the objection or the misunderstanding. You may discover that the basis of the objection is something as simple as "John never saw the memo on the changes in pricing policy." Show him the memo!

Establish a parallel situation to the other party's own business or interests

If you discover a misunderstanding over the reasoning behind an idea, handle it by putting the objection into a relevant context for them, using their experience. "Let me put it another way. Using your last transaction as an example, it's as if…"

Convert the negative objection to a positive benefit

An objection is often an opportunity to reinforce a benefit to the other party. "Let's look at this another way. Joining our large network of associates works in your favor because, with our range of connections and flexibility, you can get as little or as much as you need, when you need it."

Shift the focus away from an objection to a relevant question that will be accepted in its place

Objection: "I don't like the higher fees."

Answer: "I understand that. Isn't the real question whether you feel the increased value is there for you? As we have discussed, the new arrangement provides these benefits to you…"

When all else fails, sometimes you need to revert to some old favorites:

- *Benefits outweigh disadvantages*: "I think the individual objections you've raised are well taken. However, the proposal is not unfair and the benefits far outweigh the disadvantages."
- *What is most important*: "Yes, the fees are higher than our competitors. I'm sure you'll agree what is most important is your company's ability to…and this package provides this substantial benefit to you."
- *The long run*: "In the short run there may be a slight disadvantage. This is more than compensated by the critical benefits to you in the long run."
- *Nothing is perfect*: "You're right. This proposal is not as generous as you were expecting. Under these circumstances, no proposal would be significantly more to your liking. This one gives you three really vital benefits that you need immediately, namely…"
- *Humor*: Use humor *only* if you know the objection is trivial. Be careful about this because, if you are not sure, you trivialize the other person's concern and it is likely they will take it personally. Not good.

A note about humor: I advise you to be cautious, and when in doubt, don't. However, I have seen humor work in three different ways.

- *When it adds perspective.* If you make a comment that reminds people of the world outside it can soothe tempers. For example, in a discussion about the speed of receiving email, you could say something like "Still beats snail mail."
- *When it is self-deprecating.* Making a joke at your own expense shows that you don't take yourself too seriously. An apology coupled with self-deprecating humor could be something like "I apologize. I missed that point completely. Without my second cup of coffee I am considered one of the walking dead."

- *Using flattery.* Be sure you are genuine about this and that it is not a context where you could get in trouble for lack of political correctness.

If you don't know the answer...

If by chance you don't know the answer, don't panic! It's okay not to know and admitting that you don't certainly trumps making something up. The problem with making things up is that it sounds as if that's what you're doing. People who make things up as a response to a question often do it as they are talking. They speak faster, and the longer they waffle on the harder it is to recover.

Try something like this instead. Say that you don't know:

- and offer to find the answer later.
- and answer a related question if relevant.
- and suggest a source where the asker might find an answer.
- and ask if anyone else in the team/group can give a brief answer.

The best answers you can give accommodate the asker and address their needs or interests in a genuine way. Being genuine about not knowing is so refreshing in a world that worships subject-matter experts!

Tension Situation Two: Deadlocks

I often hear the words stalemate and deadlock being used interchangeably. Stalemate is a chess position where one player can only move the king and the king can only move into check, which isn't allowed. Game over. The reason I mention it is that often the words are used as if they meant the same thing, yet in fact they mean something very different. "Stalemate" means the end, and the game ends without a winner. "Deadlock" means an opportunity has presented itself.

A deadlock typically arises when negotiators stop making progress and neither side sees a practical or workable path forward. It can be a catalyst for another round of discussions. However, it often isn't, because there has been a failure to agree and both parties are digging their heels in, waiting for the other to give in. No one does, so we have a deadlock.

Often one side will panic and start conceding. Before that happens, here are some alternatives to try. Above all, stay calm.

- Indicate your willingness to continue to communicate until an agreement can be reached.
- Remind both parties of common goals/purposes, needs, and the long-term benefits of working out an agreement.
- Don't get into an argument, become critical, or blame anyone.
- Repeat your position and add new evidence or support or a new angle.
- Ask the other party how you could rework your proposal/idea to make it more inclusive of their interests/needs/wants.
- Try to discuss the underlying principles or interests involved. Try to show them how an alternative solution gives them what they need. Make sure this solution still has benefit to you as well!
- Re-present one idea at a time. Then check to be sure that each idea has been clearly understood before you proceed to the next. Be alert to gray areas, such as opinions or topics that need more factual back-up.
- Probe further to understand why the other side is taking this position.
- Suggest a break so there is time to think and consider what has been said. During the break, if necessary speak to the person who won't budge or is causing a distraction. Possibly change to a different place and spend time not talking about the negotiation.
- Better yet, build breaks into your negotiation from the start. This works well because there are natural breaks expected and people are more paced and refreshed.
- Change the subject to more easily resolved issues and return to the deadlocked ones later. "Let's keep moving and set this aside for now and come back to it." This option is also known as the "set-aside" and is a subtle way to reset the agenda – you

can hopefully agree on a few less sticky issues before you come back to the deadlock.

- Agree in principle. If you agree in principle then you both at least agree with the objectives.
- Offer a minor (pre-planned) concession as a gesture.
- Suggest that each of you trades a concession.
- Concede and take an I.O.U. or a "rain-check" for a further concession.
- Suggest another meeting at a later date.
- Invite a mediator to facilitate a compromise.
- Try joint fact-finding. This can take the focus off the differences and put it on agreement about how to gather and interpret information about the negotiation. Be sure you use unbiased expert advice.
- Use humor to break the tension (but use it carefully – see above).
- Walk away (but only if you mean it – see under *Tactics*, below).

If you can take a deadlock and turn it around into a successful negotiation for both parties, the result can be powerful. It can feel as if both of you have come back from the edge of an abyss.

Tension Situation Three: Tactics

Tactics are specific behaviors with a specific objective. In a negotiation, they are generally used to deliberately affect the way the other party feels about how things might turn out. "If I put on my poker face, they won't be able to see how I feel" or "If I laugh, I'll look tougher and they'll know how silly I think their opening offer sounds" or "But Dad said we could have ice-cream" (said to Mother when he is not there, nor is it likely he said it).

What actions you take or behaviors you choose in the context of a negotiation affect the dynamics – in other words, how people feel and their willingness to continue at any given moment. The tactics can be verbal or non-verbal, often subtle and sometimes unconscious. You are not always aware you are using them and you are not always aware of how they are affecting you or others. This means they can work for or against you, whether you know it or not. So, it's best to be aware and choose your behaviors wisely and consistently.

The good news: tactics don't have power over you if you recognize them for what they are.

A common mistake negotiators make is to understand their *positions* on each issue without considering what they want their *tactics* to be. As a result, their behavior is inconsistent with what they say they want to achieve. For example, you claim to care about preserving the relationship but you are acting like a jackass. A gap is created by what you want and what others perceive.

This happens because of bad preparation and the fact that most of us have two or three favorite behaviors or tactics we default to under pressure. These go-to tactics get used again and again. For example, using exaggerated opening positions, being secretive about interests, or deferring to an absent third party ("I can't do anything until I have talked to my partner").

At the same time, each of us is vulnerable to certain tactics that are used towards us; we need to be aware of these and protect ourselves from reacting inappropriately to them. For example, some people give in or concede if someone is overly enthusiastic or excited or kind, or if they use tears or yell or use aggressive behavior. Think about what your go-to tactics are as well as the tactics you can't resist responding to. It is eye-opening.

So, how you behave affects how people feel about you and the possible outcome of the negotiation. Here are some examples of tactics that you can use if you want to communicate that you are helpful, willing, and collaborative:

- Express confidence and desire to achieve a mutually beneficial outcome.
- Make minor concessions to show a spirit of cooperation.
- Concede the obvious when you are wrong.
- Create alternative solutions.
- Reveal your interests early.
- Provide plenty of relevant information and facts.
- Prevent interruptions.
- Come to the negotiation fully prepared and keep good notes.

- Choose a time and place that are comfortable for both parties.
- Acknowledge and praise where due.
- Listen without interrupting.
- Probe and identify real interests.
- Make enough time for the negotiation.
- Educate gently when you hear an unrealistic expectation.
- Propose a separate brainstorming session if necessary.
- Emphasize shared interests and the history of agreements between you.
- Help the other not to lose face.
- Avoid threats, cynicism, and offensive behavior.
- Work to create good chemistry.
- Invite others to build on your ideas.
- Summarize where it makes sense to show you understand.

Positive, affirming, and cooperative tactics can create a sense of wellbeing and enthusiasm for the outcome of the negotiation and how the other party feels about you. They are ways to manage tension, after all. However, keep in mind that not all positive behaviors are what you think they are. A reminder not to take anything personally, even the good stuff. A famous dog-trainer told me once, "You can't always trust a wagging tail." With that in mind, a positive tactic that a well-known and high-profile property developer in the US uses to gain advantage during negotiations when he wants to buy a business is to instruct his staff to inform the team waiting outside his office that he is very busy, that they won't be able to stay long, and that he won't shake their hand (apparently he doesn't do hand-shaking). Then when he enters the room, the team members are charmed by his hand-shaking and friendliness and exclusive one-hour conversation about business and glossed-over terms of sale. They feel flattered and sought-after and in reality have been duped, giving the glossy property developer the upper hand.

There may be times when you want to communicate a tough or competitive approach to some issues. Remember, you can be tough and honest, or tough for the right reasons. You can also be tough for the wrong reasons! I recommend taking the high road and not wasting your time with tactics like lies, false promises, or behaviors that create animosity or fear – no matter how tempting it may be to indulge in these. You need to consider the impact of such behaviors on your relationship with the other party. Be mindful also that others may use these tactics on you.

- Using self-serving compromises or false or exaggerated concessions.
- Being poker-faced.
- Tricking others into revealing their position first.
- "Hesitating" before conceding.
- Surprising the other party by adding a new member to the team.
- Inflating your real needs.
- Showing outrage in order to gain a concession.
- Pretending that a fair offer is unacceptable so you drive a harder bargain.
- Deferring to an absent third party when there isn't one.
- Pushing for a quick close when the other party hasn't had time to read or digest all the information.
- Changing the rules to suit yourself.
- Bluffing e.g. "This is my final offer."
- Lying.
- Withholding or slanting information.
- Using a two-on-one approach – two of you against one of them.
- Using good-guy, bad-guy.
- Giving a false promise of future business.
- Delaying to irritate or gain advantage.
- Chipping away at the agreement.
- Unfairly influencing the other party's perception of the bargaining range ("There's not a lot of wiggle room here" or "This could go anywhere. The possibilities are limitless").
- Name-dropping, posing, posturing, or a show of wealth ("I don't need this negotiation").
- Building in a large "cushion" or an exaggerated opening position.

The list can go on and on. So what can you do to take the power away from a tactic if it is used against you? Whether the tactic is cooperative and positive or competitive and negative, it is always good practice to check it if you have a hunch that you should. Here are some sample responses if you are on the receiving end:

- Ignore it. They may just be testing you or winding you up.
- Ask a positive question about why they are doing or saying the particular thing.
- Expose the tactic. Tell them you know what they are doing and you'd like them to stop.
- Do a tit-for-tat. Give as good as you get.
- Stall for time to give yourself a chance to form your response. Can be minutes, hours, or days.
- Walk out (though think carefully before doing this – it is hard to walk back if you were wrong about it being a tactic).

Remember that you always have a choice to continue a negotiation or not. I hope you choose not to accept abusive or unethical behavior, even when the cost of walking away seems high.

Sometimes the behavior is bad but forgivable. Done once, you may empathize with them. We are all human. Done twice, sympathize perhaps. Recognize it as bad planning. A third time, not so sure. As Ian Fleming wrote in *Goldfinger*, "Once is happenstance, twice is coincidence, three times it is enemy action."

Your best bet is that if you encounter bad behavior, call it for what it is.

Cicero said, "If you have no basis for an argument, abuse the plaintiff."

Is this who you want to negotiate with?

Tension is a natural part of life and it is both friend and foe depending on how you deal with it. The Nimble Negotiator expects it and embraces its inevitability.

five

Your Nimble Negotiation Style

This above all; to thine own self be true.

William Shakespeare

Your Nimble Negotiation style is a bit like your wardrobe. Hopefully you choose a sweater if it's cold, a heavier jacket and gloves if it is raining or snowing, a light shirt if it's hot. Just like the old saying, "There's no such thing as bad weather, just bad clothes."

We all have a natural communication style that we adopt most of the time. It influences how we negotiate. How others perceive us, as well as how we build rapport and relationships, and even how we behave under pressure. The same tendencies and preferences that make you good or bad as a communicator make you good or bad as a negotiator. It is when you can recognize your own style, and then adapt to others, that your communication with them will foster understanding and cooperation.

There is a lot written about different negotiation and communication styles, which I encourage you to explore. What is consistent throughout the literature is the need to be aware of your own proclivity towards a set of behaviors most of the time, and particularly under pressure. Understanding this makes negotiating a little easier and you are likely to get better outcomes as a result.

Confrontation or conflict is more likely during a negotiation because of the tension usually associated with it. It is also important that you consider what happens to your communication style under these circumstances.

Nimble Negotiating shines a light on becoming comfortable with confrontation. Few of us are perfectly at ease telling others what we think when we think it needs to be said, or overtly disagreeing. We are concerned about hurting feelings, insulting someone, or the myriad of other emotions that result from our experience with confrontation.

Add that to the tension that comes from the "give and take over who gets what" of negotiation and your ability to confront takes on a special importance. At the core of being a Nimble Negotiator is being comfortable with confrontation.

Most people associate confrontation with something negative. The Nimble Negotiator sees confrontation as an opportunity. An opportunity to clarify understanding, deepen your relationships, and add value to both sides in your negotiations. Often negotiation starts with the idea that we are all on different sides. One will win and one will lose. What if there are no sides?

In a negotiation, you don't have to choose between being open, honest, and direct and achieving a good outcome for yourself. There is nothing stopping you from the possibility of having both.

As a Nimble Negotiator, your goal is to find a way to talk about the issues that are most important to both sides in a neutral and respectful way. A little confrontation for the purposes of clarity, early in your planning and throughout your negotiation, makes the biggest difference to your negotiation outcome.

Let me give you some important principles to keep in mind about confrontation:

- Don't take it personally. Whatever the other person thinks or feels, it is not your problem. It is their problem, because it is their way of looking at the world. They see the world through their eyes. It is up to you to decide whether or not you want to get involved in someone else's problems.
- You are entitled to your own opinions and feelings and to express them to others.
- You are entitled to ask for what you want, although you should realize the other person is entitled to refuse you.

- You are entitled to change your mind.
- You are entitled to achieve your goals and aspirations as long as you do not take advantage of someone else.
- Sometimes the decisions you make will be the wrong ones. So what? Learn from them and try again.

Understanding your confrontation style

Understanding your own style and the style of the people or individuals you are dealing with will add a powerful element of control and confidence.

I think the best way to become a Nimble Negotiator is to take a fresh look at your negotiating style and, in particular, how you handle confrontation. I have covered communication behavior and confrontation styles extensively in my last two books. This time I will focus on how you can use your confrontation style to be a Nimble Negotiator.

One of the Nimble Negotiator's primary goals when they negotiate is clarity. Without clarity we are making assumptions about the other party, creating tension, not listening, and very likely wasting time.

Seeking clarity often requires confrontation. It means that you may need to have the courage to stop the flow of a conversation at an inconvenient time, go back over something others think is obvious, ask a question at a critical juncture or when you think it might not be the right question or think it is too late. Trust your instincts: if the issue is not clear to you, that's enough. It may not be clear to others, either.

Here are some sample phrases you can use for clarifying:

- If I understand you correctly, you mean/this means/it means…
- Let's see if I understand/understand you…
- Do you/Does this mean then that…?
- So what you are really saying is…
- Would it be correct to say that…?
- So in other words…
- Can I conclude from this that…?
- What if…?
- May I assume that…?
- Am I right in assuming…?

- If I may interject for a moment...
- May I interject?

I know this is not easy. You won't always get it right – most of us don't. Clarity is the holy grail of communication. If in the future you only get it right more often than you did in the past, you are making great strides.

Your personal negotiating style has a strong influence on your approach to negotiation and choice of tactics. You are more likely to behave in a way that has "worked for you in the past" or feels easiest for you when you are under pressure.

As I discussed in Chapter Three, negotiators often approach negotiating by preparing their tactics depending on how they want to manage an issue. For example, will they be "submissive" or "aggressive" during the discussion about price or be "compromising" on timing? Perhaps they'll be "accommodating" on issues around design specifications and "avoiding" if the issue of our impending merger comes up? Other possibilities include "competing", "collaborating", "team-building", "friendly", and "indifferent".

This type of "mood and tone" planning around individual issues is a good way to prepare. There are benefits to identifying the key negotiation issues and also aligning yourself (or the team) around how to behave consistent with the agreed tone and mood.

The negotiating archetypes

But no matter how well you plan, you come to the negotiating table with a propensity to behave a certain way, particularly when you are under pressure. If you are aware of this in yourself you will have a more refined ability to observe it in others, which in turn means you can prepare better, flex, and respond more appropriately. Better for you and for them. A richer understanding of each other means better negotiating outcomes.

There are many schools of thought about personal style and behavior that I would encourage you to explore. As a guide, I'll refer to four negotiating styles and their archetypes: the Ruler, the Sage, the Caregiver, and the Magician.

Archetypes describe recurring patterns of behavior that are present in all of us. Jung identified 12 of them and these are worth exploring for your own insight. I have chosen these four because they are easiest to observe and because I have encountered them most often in negotiations. I'll align these with negotiating behavior and show how each of us has a propensity to lean in to a style.

You may recognize yourself in these archetypes. Most of us have several archetypes at play but generally only one dominates. Keep in mind that I am not trying to put you in a box. The key is to recognize the propensities in ourselves and others and to use our observations and responses to build understanding.

The Ruler (consistent with: Command and Control, or Driver)

This is a negotiating style preferred by people who are comfortable with confrontation and see it as a sport – an essential part of negotiation. You'll recognize them as people who can come across as impatient, abrupt, or straightforward. They have a strong concern for outcomes, form strong positions, and tend to speak using statements and conclusions rather than questions. They can dominate meetings or conversations and, in the extreme, are loud, pushy, and intimidating. This type of behavior can create aggression in others and lead to breakdowns in communication. People who default to this style find it difficult to take their finger off the trigger and end up applying the same intensity to every issue, whether it is important or trivial. The problem with this approach is that trampling on someone's self-respect it is not conducive to cooperation or collaboration.

The Ruler can also rely heavily on formality. This means they are neither friendly nor unfriendly and are highly structured and disciplined. The authoritarian side of Ruler behavior can be time-consuming and laborious and very much about sticking to the rules. It is important to this style to avoid chaos.

Because of their desire to exercise power and their relative comfort with intimidating behavior, Rulers can also default to approaches that have short-term results. Relationships can be eroded and walkouts are more likely to occur.

On the bright side, sometimes this behavior can force concessions and accelerate the process if there is a sense of urgency or the other side is less prepared or "weak". The Ruler is a good person to have on your team if the other side is aggressive.

Your reconnaissance calls or meetings to the Ruler should avoid small talk and be very up-front about what you want to achieve.

If you want to negotiate well with the Ruler:
- Be brief in your discussions, proposals, questions, and negotiations, but have the details ready.
- Don't make excuses (a good rule anyway but particularly important with Rulers).
- Preparation is critical, so be extra thorough with your homework.
- Know what you want and be prepared to state it early. Back it up – succinctly and specifically.
- As you describe your proposals, make your point first, and then explain the detail.
- Be direct and well structured – if you disagree, tell them and ask them to explain their views further.
- Avoid sounding upset or angry.
- Conclude the negotiation by restating what you have resolved/ agreed and next steps.
- Maintain eye contact; keep your body upright and relaxed.
- Make any written communication short and to the point.
- Answer questions in a brief and specific way.

See Chapter Four on Managing Tension for specific responses to aggression or bullying.

The Sage (consistent with Rationalize, Employ Logic and Order, or Analytical)

The Sage has an analytical mind that is acutely interested in the *process* of negotiating. As negotiators, Sages methodically explore options, have a strong need for facts and detail, and require time for analysis and consideration. They are the expert, scholar, and detective. Their desire is to understand the world through intelligence and analysis.

You may recognize them as fairly physically low-key. During a negotiation, they are the ones sitting quietly or performing a specific task of "backing up" an argument when called upon. They may also be overly critical. They are usually very uncomfortable with confrontation and tend to show little emotion. This doesn't mean they don't feel it, they just don't show it. Because of this, it may be more difficult to discover their real needs.

Under pressure, Sages can slip into being verbal bullies, although they rarely exaggerate or name-call: their bullying will feel more like stubbornness. Be aware that their keen sense of process and discomfort with confrontation sometimes leads them to hide behind the rules. They can get bogged down in details and create frustration and delays. Beware of being underprepared, because it is difficult to claw back credibility with this type. In the moment you may be forced to concede because you don't have facts or analysis available.

Like the Ruler, the Sage can also default to formality and being judgmental. Neither friendly nor unfriendly, black and white and focused on the process. In a negotiation, this formality may make it more difficult to uncover real needs.

Sages sometimes bring surprises to the table in terms of creative solutions. They have usually thought deeply about most aspects of a problem and are a good source of alternatives. However, their relative comfort with sticking to the rules may mean that creativity is compromised.

Your reconnaissance calls or meetings with the Sage can be rationalized by focusing on ensuring complete understanding of the key issues, any obstacles that need to be faced, and alternatives to explore. Ask what they understand about the issues, seek their opinion, and find out if they think any issues are more important than others. You may need to send an agenda ahead for the meeting and ask for corrections and clarifications to further understanding.

If you want to negotiate well with the Sage:
- Be sure your homework is accurate and complete; have facts and data ready to discuss.
- Facts and real examples resonate with the Sage, so make them your first choice of support for your arguments.

- Demonstrate your understanding of the issues and, where possible, paraphrase back to them. If you disagree, say so and explain why.
- Don't rush them, take your time, and let them take theirs.
- Don't exaggerate or use sweeping statements.
- Be low-key in your style, careful, thoughtful, not perky.
- Don't answer questions too quickly or interrupt.

The Caregiver (consistent with Amiable/Social or Get Friendly, Seek Harmony)

Negotiating is a challenging task for this type, generally speaking. They are uncomfortable with confrontation and competition over resources, and like negotiations to be fair and harmonious. Caregivers would prefer not to fight because relationships and cooperation are important to them. They are loyal supporters and skilled empathizers. They are also sympathetic, patient, and usually reasonable. Because of this, they can be found to hold back or not speak up for themselves in a negotiation. As a result, they may hold some resentment, frustration, or anger if their issues or concerns are not recognized or addressed. I have seen Caregivers unravel and pick apart a deal afterwards, if they are not happy with it. Just because they didn't speak up, don't assume they are satisfied. It could also mean that there are delays or procrastination due to discomfort with handling confrontation.

Caregivers can also default to friendliness or rescuing in a negotiation. They may talk a lot in an attempt to diffuse tension and make a genuine effort to create a positive atmosphere.

Their intentions and behaviors can create long-term solutions and classic win-win outcomes. However, sometimes Caregivers can encourage bullies and not get their rightful share.

Reconnaissance calls or meetings and negotiations with this type can include discussions that are not about the negotiation at all. Talk about opinions, feelings, and concerns. Show genuine curiosity, learn about their life and interests, share some of yours, make a little more time for conversations, and focus on how the outcomes can benefit the overall goal. Reconnaissance goes a long way toward avoiding unpleasant surprises or embarrassment. This is appealing to the Caregiver.

If you want to negotiate well with the Caregiver:
- Occasionally have your meetings at a neutral place. Take a walk, go to a coffee shop, and keep it informal.
- Avoid judgments as you describe issues and challenges.
- Say how challenges or obstacles make you feel.
- Recommend solutions, ask for their ideas, and offer to help if needed.
- Be warm, friendly, and talkative.
- Show you are interested in how others feel.
- Talk about your personal experience where relevant.

The Magician (Consistent with Expressive, and Feel it and Say it)

This archetype is comfortable with self-expression and at the same time fragile, as they can easily take confrontation as a blow to the ego. As negotiators, they are generally articulate under pressure and have a high level of energy and enthusiasm. This can be positive and motivating but, if not organized and managed, can lead to misfires and deadlocks. They particularly fear unintended negative consequences and are vocal about being keen to find solutions that are fair and beneficial to both parties.

Cooperation always feels better than a stalemate to a Magician, so their enthusiasm and energy to "get things done" can be interpreted as accommodating or compromising. This is good if it is true. Magicians, however, need to be careful not to appear manipulative by making sure their desire for the "grand scheme" and to turn "vision into reality" stays grounded, pragmatic, and within the bounds of the negotiation. The irony of the Magician is that the very enthusiasm that drives their negotiation approach can lead to a disconnection with reality or drama and stalemate.

Your reconnaissance calls or meetings need to be done with the big picture in mind. State your goal of wanting to create clarity and understanding on key issues and explore alternatives. Acknowledge the positive aspects of their contribution.

If you want to negotiate well with the Magician:

- Make sure they understand the implications and importance of what they are doing, and how they fit into the wider objective.
- Be direct, positive, use facts and examples.
- Avoid being overtly judgmental.
- Make recommendations and/or ask how they would like to solve or address the problem/issue/obstacle.
- Try to appear confident and dynamic.
- Don't compete.
- Be spontaneous, suggest something different.

Look for clues

Recognizing negotiation styles must become central to your preparation. You'll do well if you improve your ability to prepare and respond appropriately. You will likely meet people who seem to have a combination of styles. Some people who tend to be very aggressive or dominating can be very expressive and big-picture oriented. In the same way, those who dislike confrontation can be very direct. Some combinations don't work, though. The Caregiver is rarely if ever intimidating or pushy and the Sage is rarely overtly expressive.

Because it isn't always obvious which type or mix of types someone is, take your time and look for clues when assessing how to negotiate with them.

Sages and Magicians often find it hardest to engage with each other. Same with Rulers and Caregivers. The gaps are challenging but not impossible to fill. Recognizing someone's archetype isn't a guarantee that your negotiation will go well, but it will give you an advantage. You'll feel more confident and in control, as well as being able to respond to them in a way that will help you get the outcome you want.

What about a Nimble archetype?

The Nimble archetype has a strong intention to seek balanced and fair negotiation solutions where possible. They know their negotiation advantage comes from excellent preparation, increased self-awareness, respect for others, and a willingness to compromise. As a result they:

- Have a readiness to ask and answer direct and open enquiry. They listen more than they talk.
- Are prepared to take reasonable risks and, if it doesn't work out, not to take anything too personally. They care, but not too much.
- Attach a strong value to keeping promises.
- Avoid negativity and focus instead on mutual benefit with reasonable hopes of addressing all concerns.
- Lean towards a tough-but-fair negotiation approach.
- Make the effort to create an environment for open, honest communication.
- Are prepared to work around deadlocks and obstacles.
- Are pragmatic and succinct.
- Think "us against the problem" not "you vs. me".

This may sound as if we are describing the patron saint of negotiation. Not the case. The Nimble archetype faces the same challenges, fears, and aspirations as every other archetype. We are all human. Because of this, we are also all capable of a better way.

six

The Magic of Opening Positions

The opening is the only phase that holds the potential for
true creativity and doing something entirely new.
Gary Kasparov

This chapter is about the importance and nature of opening positions and how to prepare for them and respond to them. Opening positions in a negotiation are best captured by the old saying, "The beginning is half of the whole." This is an inescapable truth about negotiating.

Your opening position is that point in the negotiation where you get around to saying what you want or what you are prepared to do. You put your stake in the ground. It represents the sum total of your preparation and what you think is the best possible outcome that you can get. A well-reasoned and strong opening position will allow you to work your way more easily to common ground with the other party, so you eventually and ideally arrive at a place where you both feel satisfied.

Common ground is generally considered to be where the two sides' interests overlap. Sounds easy enough. I wish. Often negotiators are not clear on what they actually want, or what the best possible outcome could be. They don't know enough about the other side to know what they can get. This makes the whole process more difficult than it needs to be.

What happens during the opening part of the negotiation, without a doubt, affects the rest of it. It is the place where you set the groundwork for how easily and quickly you will reach agreement or find a solution. As a Nimble Negotiator, your goal in your opening position is to be well informed and prepared, firm on your interests, but flexible about how to achieve them. You can't know it all, however carefully you have done your reconnoitering and planning. You will learn more about the other party as you start to negotiate.

Here are some points to keep in mind as you prepare your opening position.

Use the power of alternatives

Part of what makes you feel confident that your opening position is strong and relevant is knowing what you'll do if you fail to reach agreement with the other party. We all have alternatives – whether or not we like them is something else. If you put some effort into identifying them you'll find you are a little more relaxed. One option is not to negotiate: a key source of power in any negotiation is your ability to walk away. More positively, your alternatives can also be a fertile ground for creativity. Authors Fisher and Ury have called knowing your alternatives a BATNA – Best Alternative to a Negotiated Agreement.

A few things to be aware of about BATNAs:

- They are constantly changing. Remember, "The opera is not over until the fat lady sings." It is easy to feel confident because you have two offers on your car this week. By next week it could be down to one – or none. Keep an open mind, have other options, and keep playing the field until the deal is done.
- Be careful not to reveal your BATNA. If you do, the other party has no incentive to offer you any more.
- Don't lie about your BATNA. A friend's mother was selling her house in France and told a prospective buyer a lie about another offer she claimed to have had. He called her bluff and a year later when the house was still not sold he came back with another offer, even lower than his original one. Fabricating has lots of other problems associated with it – ethical, moral, legal, and face-saving – so just don't go there!

- Quantify your BATNA. Not every issue has a number attached to it, but you should try to give it a "go-no-go" position. This means that point where you are ready to decide to proceed or not. The go-no-go position is also called your reservation point. Having a reservation point can help quantify what matters to you personally.

  For example, I often use temporary private accommodation rather than hotels when I am travelling in and out of cities for short visits. This is generally cheaper and, because I can choose from many options, some nearer to my clients, I can reduce the amount of driving time I have to and from various meetings. For me, it is a quality-of-life issue. It enables me to spend more time working from my home office, have extra time with my family, exercise more regularly, and eat healthier food than I can get on the road.

  Because I can plan ahead several weeks and guarantee I'll be staying for a number of consecutive nights, I ask for a discount on the rate. If my first choice doesn't want to discount, I have an alternative or two that would satisfy me. I have come up with a number that feels right to me.

Having a BATNA gives you the confidence to walk away or choose the next best alternative. It may not be your preferred option, but it's one you can accept. That's the power of alternatives.

To open or not to open: the answer is yes

You can be forgiven for being a little confused or wary about opening positions because there is some disagreement and a lot of discussion about how they should be presented. Do you go first or is it better to wait until the other side tells you what they want? Conventional negotiating wisdom actively warns negotiators against stating their opening position first. "Don't show your cards or let the other side know what you are thinking."

The crazy thing about this is if everyone did it, you'd end up with no one saying anything and nothing would ever get done. What's more, we have all become so accustomed to the logic that no one is going to accept our opening position that we whip it up by "shooting for more" than we expect to get. At the same time, the other side is typically doing the same thing in the opposite direction. While you are exaggerating to protect your interests, you need to be careful not to exaggerate so much that you offend the other person. Sounds like tricky territory.

The Nimble Negotiator likes stating their opening position first. Why? Because going first and doing it well carries a lot of weight in a negotiation. Of course there may be the rare time when it is not possible or in your interests to go first (we'll talk about that later), but research conducted by Adam Galinsky and Tomas Mussweiler found that 85% of the time the first offer will predict the outcome of a negotiation. Remember also, as we saw earlier, that if you reveal your interests early, you double the probability that the other party will reveal theirs. This speaks volumes for transparency and directness.

The anchoring effect

There is also a phenomenon called the "anchoring effect". Essentially, it means that people will generally make judgments based on your opening position and will adjust their response upward or downward from there but, interestingly, not by much. This is because we tend to rely heavily on the first piece of information offered, whether it is right or wrong, ridiculous or real. The anchoring effect is used around us every day.

For example, if a car has a sticker price for $30,000 and you negotiate to buy it for $25,000, you believe you got a good deal, even if $25,000 is more than you originally intended to pay.

Or your daughter wants a new pair of jeans and finds an expensive pair on sale for $150. Your quiet "No" brings more pleading insistence from your teenager. She continues, "Here is a pair for $120. There's a special on this pair – if we buy two, the second pair is 33% off. For $200 we get two pairs, that makes it a real bargain!"

It applies to something as simple as a carton of milk on sale or as complicated as leasing an oil rig.

Communication anchors

The anchoring effect also applies to how you communicate. This affects emotions, perceptions, and expectations, not just the numbers.

It is like the old saying, "You never get a second chance to make a first impression." How you communicate has an anchoring effect on how others feel about your opening position. Not surprisingly, the same applies to how you respond to someone else's opening.

The most common communication anchors I see stem from nervous tension. For example, in an effort to come across as tough, fearless, or confident, you may appear over-confident or inflexible. If you are worried about being tricked or taken advantage of, you may inadvertently adopt an aggressive tone of voice and body posture, making you appear difficult to deal with. If you lack confidence or feel intimidated, you may not be assertive or clear in expressing your interests and end up looking uncertain or vulnerable. If you are not listening or are distracted, you may miss an important clue about how the other person feels or thinks and come across as indifferent or uninformed. You may not like or trust the other person and be guarded about what you share, making you appear secretive. The point about impressions is that they don't have to be right to matter.

Even enthusiasm, well intended as it may seem, can be misinterpreted. My client Mark is a high-energy, very expressive and positive person. During the planning and initial reconnaissance conversations in a recent negotiation with potential suppliers, one party took his enthusiasm to mean he was excited about their deal (which he was), flexible on his terms (which he was a little), and more interested in working with them than with anyone else (which he wasn't). Mark is just nice to everybody. When it came time to present opening positions, the other party was visibly surprised and embarrassed by how badly they had misread the situation. They had started out comfortable and confident, believing they were Mark's top choice among the competing suppliers and a ringer to win the business. They delivered their opening position with such confidence based on their misunderstanding of the situation and showed such a gap in understanding that they weren't even considered for the short list.

I was involved in the negotiation of an office rent renewal for a non-profit in London. The landlord kept us waiting at the start of the meeting and, when he arrived, his tone was aggressive from the beginning; he asserted that the market rent he could be getting in a new arrangement was far more than we were paying. This was before we said anything of substance. Because of his abrupt tone and aggressive behavior, we felt the negotiation was over before it began. We left the meeting feeling as if we should pursue alternative accommodation, which we did.

Another client was recently surprised by an opening position in the form of an extreme price increase from one of their major suppliers.

Instead of a shocked response like "How could you take advantage of us like this? You know we have a lot of pressure on our margins already!", they responded, "We value our long-term relationship, as we believe you do. This price increase comes as a big surprise to us – without warning or explanation. We'd appreciate hearing more about what's behind it."

So, your tone and actions act like an anchor for the rest of the negotiation. It's best to communicate your opening position (or respond to the other party's) in a way that demonstrates understanding, matches your intention and goals, and is backed up with relevant facts, data, and insight. (More on how to make your messages more persuasive using facts, data, and insight in Chapter Seven.)

Expect uncertainty

While it is important to do as much insight-gathering as possible beforehand, you can still only learn certain aspects about the other person/party when you are actually negotiating with them. As you negotiate you learn.

There will always be a certain amount of uncertainty built into negotiation, and a need for you to do your best in the moment. Relying on your best skills as a Nimble Negotiator will help you navigate uncertainty. Success starts with expecting uncertainty as a certainty!

Keep calm, stay focused and direct. If you need to ask clarifying questions, do it in a way that compels the other person to answer, but also makes it easy for them to do so. Even in less-than-optimal situations, you can still resist being strong-armed into blurting out a less-than-optimal opening position. (As a good rule of thumb, always write your opening position down, just in case you get rattled.)

It is critical that when you make your opening position, it doesn't sound like a demand. You can be confident and clear. For example:

- In the spirit of clarity and expediency, I have prepared a set of terms that would be acceptable to me. I appreciate that your terms may be different. Let's use these as a starting point and explore from there. I'd love to hear your ideas.

Or:

- Thank you for the effort your team has put into this meeting. I have prepared an outline of what would work for me. I know your terms may be a bit different and I am interested in exploring how we can work together.

The reality is, most people have not prepared their opening position, or even a way of saying it that sets the tone for the negotiation in a thoughtful way.

Welcome going second

Let's say someone jumps in and makes their opening position before you do. No problem. Being Nimble means you prefer first and also welcome going second.

A good anchoring response would be, "Thank you for sharing your thoughts with me. I have also spent some time preparing some terms that would work for me, and I would like to share those with you now. I have to say, though, my terms are very different from what you have just mentioned. I'm ready to discuss everything openly and fully."

It is likely that there will be an opportunity to clarify and learn more. A great way to continue the opening position conversation is to explore priorities. This enables you to learn without it feeling as if you are prying and, importantly, to learn about broader interests, like what is most important and why. Use formulae like:

- For me, Issue A is more important than B.
- John, of these three conditions, which is the most important to you?
- Why is that?
- What would give you more value, increasing A or B?

- If I were to forego the timing constraints on Issue A, would that be better for you?
- How can I make that easier for you?
- Are there any other criteria that will influence your decision?
- If you were to rank-order those criteria, which would be first and second?

The key is to make sure you understand the other party's opening position before you continue. Don't make your opening position before you are ready.

For example, their opening may give you a new insight that potentially alters your position. If you can, ask for time to think about or digest what you have learned. You may want to give a more thoughtful response. My friend Erica's boss asked if she would consider applying for an exciting new position that was opening up in her division at work. The answer was yes! However, after the second interview, she learned the job would be moved overseas in the near term, meaning she would have to live in Munich for a few years. This new information about the company's opening position caused her to change her mind and withdraw her expression of interest.

The multiple-offer approach

This is an approach that will help you shape an opening position better when you have many issues to consider at one time.

A good way to "digest" and address multiple issues is first to prioritize them, then give each one a percentage weight, and finally, after some soul searching, see if you can come up with say three alternatives to propose that would work for you.

One of my clients told me the story of his wife, Katie, and her negotiation with a university that offered her a new teaching position in their biochemistry program. Late on in the interview the human resources officer asked her about her salary history (she was returning to work after having four children). Instead of addressing the issue and setting an anchor, she said, "Let's see if we are a good fit for each other before we discuss that."

The interview ended well and she had a few days to think about whether or not to accept the job.

There were many things she needed to consider before she could make up her mind. She began by "unbundling" the key issues and prioritizing them. When that was complete, she decided to construct an opening position that had three alternatives.

Here's how she did it.

Salary was important to Katie, but given that she had a family of young children there were other things to consider: work hour flexibility (her husband works full time), ability to do private consulting (she helps parents of special needs children with dietary counseling), and paid sabbatical (she's writing a book with a publishing deadline). So Katie identified flextime, salary, consulting privileges, and sabbatical as her four key issues.

Now, she had to prioritize. Here is what she came up with in percentages:

- Salary (50).
- Consulting privileges (20) – a great way to enhance her income.
- Flextime (20) – a chance to finish her book during daylight hours.
- Sabbatical (10) – an alternative way to finish the book.

After unbundling and prioritizing, the next step was to create three combinations of roughly equal value to her.

Package One
The salary that the company offered, complete flextime, unlimited consulting, and a one-month sabbatical after two years.

Package Two
Salary of 20% above what was on offer, complete flextime, consulting under control of employer, three weeks paid vacation, no sabbatical.

Package Three
Salary of 10% above what was offered, flextime of three days per week, consulting time of two days per week, three weeks paid vacation, no sabbatical.

Katie decided she felt comfortable with any of these three options and was confident about using them as her opening position. She went back to meet with the university and as a result settled on Option Three. Last news I heard was things are progressing well. She commented that the best way to finish a book is to have a plan and not enough time. Without the sabbatical in the package but with increased consulting time, she finds that the stimulation from clients is helping her creative process. The publishing deadline will be met!

Multiple options are a good way to structure your thinking around what you want as well as allowing the other party to feel as though they have choices when you are negotiating.

Open on purpose

So, you must have an opening position if you intend to negotiate.

It would make sense, then, that your opening offer should be more than an educated guess at what might be acceptable to the other side. Get insight first-hand from the people you are negotiating with. Ask. To make it work for you, you have to be well enough prepared to know what you really want and be ready to find out what works for the other party.

The most effective opening positions demonstrate understanding of both sides. Go first because you can. Be happy to go second – that's okay too. Never be strong-armed into making an opening position if you are not ready.

Done well, good opening positions will speed up the negotiation process, reduce stress, and generate better outcomes.

seven

Persuasion and Negotiation

If you would persuade, you must appeal to interest rather than intellect
Benjamin Franklin

A smart, experienced, and successful client said something to me recently that both surprised and delighted me. It was, "Why should I care about being persuasive when I'm negotiating?" As far as he was concerned, negotiating was all about the quality of the deal; by being prepared better with a smarter, tougher team you could win more often.

I love this because it illustrates an epidemic of misunderstanding in conventional negotiation and a sentiment I hear often: there is no need to be persuasive when you negotiate. In effect, the mistaken belief is that negotiation and persuasion are mutually exclusive.

I couldn't disagree more. Persuasion and negotiation are symbiotic. Adding a persuasive approach to your negotiation means you reflect an understanding of the other person, the context, and the issues. Any time you need to protect a relationship, or need the cooperation and respect of others to meet your objectives, you need to be persuasive.

If you are doing slash and burn negotiation, or don't care about any future relationship with the other person, you can skip this chapter.

So what's so good about persuasion?

Persuasive negotiating can shorten the time it takes to reach agreement, protect or enhance the quality of the relationships between negotiators, generate more creativity, and produce better outcomes – and outcomes that stick.

I believe persuasion is unwittingly left out of negotiation because it is deemed unnecessary when we are competing or trying to gain an advantage. Also, we get so wrapped up in thinking about ourselves and getting our own negotiation needs met that we focus less on the huge gains to be had by making our approach persuasive to the other party.

As I explained in Chapter Three, Step Eight of the Nimble Planning Path involves preparing questions, answers, key messages, and evidence to support your position. You may be called upon in your negotiation to reinforce the value of an alternative or an offer, change a point of view, support an outcome, position one alternative, concession or offer in relation to another, clarify misunderstanding, compel or initiate an action.

When you communicate your proposals, you must be prepared to justify or clarify them. The other party must see and appreciate how your offer benefits them. In order to do this, it is important to:

- Find out as much as you can about the *person* or *people* with whom you will be negotiating.
- Determine what is important to them and what motivates them.
- Build persuasive messages around key issues based on what you have learned in the first two steps.

Let's go into a bit more detail about what's involved in each step.

Step One: Find out as much as you can about the person or people with whom you will be negotiating

Don't put yourself in the position of trying to negotiate with someone you don't know. We often assume we understand people we are familiar with, friends, family, co-workers. Remember, you don't necessarily know how they feel about a particular issue in the context of your negotiation, so you need to look at them again through a different lens. In negotiation, assumption is a bridge to nowhere. This seems like common sense, but I am often surprised by negotiators who overlook one of the most important and basic of negotiation building blocks – understanding the other side.

Look back at the list of questions in Step One of the Planning Path (see Chapter Three). Read through the list, prioritize, and come up with whatever needs to be asked beforehand and as the negotiation evolves. If you are working with a team, sometimes it's easier to divide the relevant questions and have everyone report back with answers and ideas about what may need further exploration. Since some of the information should be gathered first-hand, decide who should be speaking with whom. It is important to "match" the person asking questions with the appropriate person on the other side. For example, don't send a young research assistant to speak to a senior executive (you'd be surprised how often this happens). If you are negotiating alone, reach out to the other side as you feel appropriate. Think about these questions and how they may help you clarify before you negotiate. Ponder them yourself, ask other people for their views and experience, continue to clarify through-out the negotiation. Knowing what you don't know and then being prepared to ask and understand are key to being persuasive as a negotiator.

The Nimble Negotiator prefers first-hand information. One of the most overlooked and best places to go for insight is the people with whom you will be negotiating. When you do this you learn more than you could ever learn from attempting to gather insight second or third-hand. You also have a chance to build rapport, observe responses, and share information. All priceless nuance!

However, this is not always possible, so instead always query your sources and double-check for the real and the imagined. Note down what you need to reality-check during the actual negotiation.

Step Two: Determine what is important to them and what motivates them

Collecting information and insight is a dynamic process and, if you are negotiating well, you will be adjusting and flexing as you need to as more insight comes to light. This next step is to work out how to position your message or offer based on what you know.

Over the years I have been able to organize de-briefing sessions with clients post-negotiation, to find out what aspects of the negotiation most affected the outcome, good or bad.

The answers help to explain why some negotiators are more successful than others, and why if you can't make an offer that is meaningful, relevant, or clear, if you can't build a relationship with the people you are engaging in negotiation, then no matter how important the negotiation issues at stake, it's not likely to go well.

The results of my research were that people's responses can be divided into three parts:

- A large proportion of the response was based on whether the other side was well organized and prepared, understood the issues, was fair, reasonable, and flexible, and had thought through alternatives.
- The next largest part of the response was based on whether they felt a personal connection and understanding with individuals on the other side of the table. Words used included liking, trust, and chemistry.

- Finally, a small fraction was based on what were described as less obvious external factors affecting the possible solutions, such as "politics" within an organization or internal processes.

There are many factors at work when we make a decision or feel persuaded by another person during a negotiation. Because of the tension involved and depending on the personal stakes, we can be on high-alert to the possibility we are being manipulated. On the other hand, we are also positively disposed and sensitive to authenticity.

Experts have classified our motivations into roughly three categories: Rational, Emotional, and Political/Cultural. These motivations exist in each of us to varying degrees, depending on the circumstances or context.

Rational

Rational motivations concern the practical and technical aspects of a decision. These might include your reservation point (your "go-no-go" number), irrefutable facts, costs, timing, price, criteria, etc. These are the "tick the box" items that "are what they are".

Emotional

Emotional motivations or needs are powerful and not often as quickly visible to us. They concern our feelings, fears, security, esteem, belonging, identity, personal fulfillment, love, and greed, to name a few.

Political/Cultural

Political/cultural motivations refer to a person's sense of power and place in their culture or organization, the need for recognition of their own language or traditions. They may also involve an internal or external factor – like politics, rules, and processes that affect "how things work" inside an organization or culture.

These influences sit alongside the personal experience and motivations of the individuals with whom you negotiate. In other words, what you learn in step one will help you create a fuller, clearer picture of what you need to emphasize as you craft your offers and positions. It is important to keep in mind that the power of persuasion lies in the relevance of your message or offer to the person or people with whom you are negotiating.

You also need to understand their sphere of influence, or authority. Find out if they make or influence the decision or if they are negotiating on behalf of someone else. Are they just collecting information to pass on to share with a person with real clout? My advice is, if at all possible, to only negotiate with people who have authority to make deals without consultation from their superiors.

You may have heard or used "I'll have to talk with my wife" or "My hands are tied." While it may be true, deferring to an absent third party is a very common way of buying time to consider and to create pressure on the other person to give us better offers.

Where possible, avoid trying to craft persuasive messages that must be "sold" to someone you know nothing about. Sometimes you have to, but in the spirit of relevance, ask a few more questions about how the decisions are made, the priority issues, and what the decision-maker's criteria are for making the decision.

Different things matter to different people.

Step Three: Build persuasive messages around key issues based on what you have learned in the two previous steps

Now, let's look at the content of your messages in the light of the research you've done.

Make sure your statement or proposal is clear, framed appropriately (see below for more about framing), and backed up with evidence.

Clarity is an underappreciated skill in negotiation. By clarity I don't necessarily mean short and to the point (although that is nice) or saying everything to ensure we miss nothing. Rather, I mean that, often because of nervous tension, people ramble or meander (take too long to get to their point) or blurt out important information too quickly. Simple messages turn into complex statements that need dissecting to be understood and as a result priorities become blurred.

Rule of thumb: say it once and say it well.

Framing

There is a phenomenon called "framing" that affects persuasiveness in negotiation. Simply put, each of us brings a different perspective to the issues at the negotiating table, so it is useful to understand how people perceive a situation, organize information, and decide what is important.

There are different types of framing that have different effects. Take the example of a person making the decision to invest in chickens so they can have their own fresh eggs for personal use. They start off wondering whether to buy at all – a frame of "chickens vs. no chickens" – and end up with many more chickens than they originally expected, and an expensive state-of-the-art chicken coop "system" due to the following forms of framing:

- Reframing the initial decision, namely buy vs. not buy chickens, to sustainable healthy home-grown nutrition vs. animal cruelty and unknown origin of food. A salesperson might say, "Producing your own eggs will obviate the need to buy unhealthy food, bring the family closer together, and encourage the kids to share responsibility by helping to raise the chickens."

- That same salesperson could then reframe this another way (called a focus frame): "People who buy this system save the cost of the system within one year by selling the extra eggs locally and never having store-bought eggs again. You can also save money and be more earth-friendly by using the fertilizer in your yard and feeding the chickens all your leftover food. Chickens also make good pets."
- Or finally (this is called a contrast frame), we can introduce the concepts of supporting the values of family togetherness, protecting the earth, and healthy nutrition: "Although the investment may seem expensive at face value, this is definitely not the case. Our installment plan means your monthly cost is equivalent to filling up the gas tank in your car. Not a lot for all the benefits this brings to your health, your family, and the planet."

Let me give you a classic example of how framing is used to shape perception. I was living in Los Angeles during the crazy time of the O.J. Simpson trial. For those of you who don't know, the former football star was accused of murdering his wife and the trial was very public. Watching it all unfold was distressing. Watching it unfold and understanding how framing was used was even more distressing!

Simply put, here's how framing was used. The judge opened the trial with O.J. innocent vs. O.J. guilty. The prosecution chose to reframe the trial as O.J. the male wife-beater vs. the female victim. The defense presented O.J. the ethnic minority victim vs. the racist police force. The frame the jury chose to adopt determined the verdict handed down. O.J. was acquitted of murder charges. Living in Los Angeles at the time and being amongst the media frenzy and the pile-of-crazy collage of public opinion, combined with the sheer horror of what had (allegedly) happened, you could see the powerful cut-through effect the framing had on the overall outcome. It distorted and oversimplified the issues, and polarized opinion.

Framing is a powerful tool. Use it compassionately.

To construct a persuasive message you need to develop the particular aspect of an issue that you feel is most important or beneficial to the other person. You could think of framing as your efforts to accentuate the positive outcome, or maximize the gain.

"Risk vs. no risk"

Psychology researchers make the case that whether people avoid or embrace risk depends on how the problem or decision is "framed".

When people are asked to choose between a sure good thing and a gamble that may lead to something more attractive, most don't want to take a risk. In my negotiating classes, when asked, about 85% of my students would rather have $10,000 for sure than a 50-50 chance of winning $20,000. In other words, most people would rather have a bird in the hand than go beating around in the bush.

However, let's turn the tables and "frame" the situation in another way. Let's take that same $10,000 and say there is a choice between losing it all and getting a 50-50 chance of losing $20,000 or nothing. Most people choose the gamble – in other words, they would choose to flip a coin and take a risk that they might lose a huge sum of money, knowing that they might end up not losing anything.

Research shows that negotiators who are put in the mindset of "cutting their losses" tend to make fewer concessions and reach more deadlocks (walk away) than negotiators who are told to "maximize gain". So, in a nutshell, the first priority is not to lose (we humans are generally loss-averse). Gains are secondary to not losing, so framing a decision in terms of possible loss is more motivating than framing it in terms of possible gain.

Dealing with framing

There are many other ways we frame – adjusting the lens through which we see the world. We have frames about ourselves and others, power and influence, stereotypes, what processes work and don't work, and many more. You are given clues by what people say to you, how they behave, and what their references are. As the saying goes, "One man's ceiling is another man's floor."

If you feel you are being manipulated by a frame, here are a few ways to counter it:

- If you hear an issue vs. issue frame, ask whether they are the real issues and then try reframing them yourself.

- Test whether the either/or or open/shut frame is valid and if it would be different if it was reframed.
- If someone stands to benefit from your decision to agree, ask them to explain how exactly.
- Always remember that anything we see on TV, radio, the web, or in print has been framed.

So, you are in charge of your own frames. You can also can affect how the other person responds to your message by the way you frame it. Framing can refresh perceptions about an issue, sharpen understanding, and bring people closer together. Be sure to test the rationale behind it if you have doubts.

Framing may also create myopia and limit your ability and sometimes willingness to see alternative viewpoints or solutions.

Almost any decision in our lives involves framing one thing relative to something else. Your ability to understand the relative importance of your position from the other person's perspective is critical. Also, beware that you too can be framed! Just as you are preparing your framing, expect that the others are too.

The right kind of support

Framing also includes choosing the most relevant support to back up your proposal or message. These are the most common types of support:

- *Facts*: make sure they are irrefutable (and true). "Our product is the least expensive on the market and rated the most reliable in bad weather"; "The ABC foundation is the only organization that provides these services to women"; "No one has visited the site."
- *Statistics*: statistics can be overused and need to be checked for their artistic merit or, rather, interpretation. For example, a statistical report showed bald heads were preferred to redheads in an online dating survey. A newspaper headline interpreted this as, "Redheaded women should shave their heads."

- *Case studies or examples*: use examples to explain who else may have done it, what they did, and the results. "X decided not to use the additional resource at first but came back for it later" or "We have used this approach for two other clients who have benefited in the following ways."
- *Demonstration*: show how your idea, product, or proposal will work. Sometimes you need to let the other party feel, touch, experience, see, and hear what you mean. "We've downloaded the software so you can use it on your system" or "Take a test drive of the car and experience it for yourself."
- *Testimonials*: who else can say this is a worthwhile or useful proposal or offer? Testimonials matter if they come from someone the other party respects or identifies with; this can be an expert, end user, industry association, or institutional body.
- *Story*: a story is "a fact wrapped in an emotion that compels us to take an action that transforms our world." Stories are a powerful tool for building understanding and usually need to contain four components if they are to work well: an emotion that comes both from the passion of the storyteller and from the reaction it elicits in the listener; a main character that the listener can identify with; a problem in the form of the adversary; and a change in the form of a redemption. Stories need time, so use them sparingly.
- *Hypothetical example*: really useful if you feel you may need to help the listener bridge from a familiar subject to a less familiar one or vice versa. Also if you need to make a complicated idea more relatable. "If you invest today, by 2019 it will have grown to…" or "Supporting this bill means your grandchildren will see salmon spawning in this river."
- *Visual aids*: where you can, illustrate or "show" something rather than try to explain it. A picture is worth a thousand words.
- *Analogy, simile, metaphor*: these are ways of explaining something by comparing it to something else. Using indirect references can be a powerful way of clarifying in negotiation, such as observing, "We are all playing on the same team" or "As far as this offer goes, there are other fish in the sea." Be sure to

clarify what they mean if you are handed one and be sure you say what you mean if you use them.

Remember that this type of support is there to help you back up what you are saying and, importantly, make your message or offer more relevant to the other person. Different types of support appeal to different types of people depending on their understanding, experience, and motivations. Keep in mind the style of the person you are negotiating with. For example, a highly analytical person would relate better to a detailed explanation than someone who is highly expressive or big-picture oriented.

Statement/offer/proposal + the right amount of the right support = relevance. Relevance is, hands-down, the most powerful persuasive tool you have. It is available to everyone.

Putting the effort into making your messages persuasive while negotiating is smart. Not just because it is the right thing to do. It demonstrates respect for the other party, shows you have the courage to be clear and transparent, and recognizes that most of the time when you negotiate you want to finish on a positive note. You never know when you may be negotiating with these people again.

eight

Games People Play

By three methods we may learn wisdom;
first by reflection, which is noblest
second by imitation, which is easiest
and third by experience, which is bitterest.

Confucius

This chapter is written in the spirit that not everyone you negotiate with is going to be Nimble or share your values of clarity and fairness.

These tips, techniques, and insights have come from the personal experience offered by my students and clients around the world, from places as far-flung as Moscow, Sydney, Beijing, Mumbai, Cairo, São Paulo, and New York. While culturally diverse, there are some common themes.

Don't settle for something worse than what you had when you started

"Our team felt under so much pressure to 'get a deal done' that we made the mistake of rushing into a decision. We were close to what we wanted, but we felt everyone had worked really hard and we were all tired. It was almost as if we didn't want to hurt the feelings of the other party, so we accepted 5% less than we should have. We should have been a little better prepared and done something as simple as writing our walk-away position down on a piece of paper."

Don't walk away unless you really mean it

"Walking away is a serious decision and one from which it is difficult to recover. Of course there will be times when you need to do it: just be sure it's what you want. I walked away from a negotiation once (because I was so aggravated), fully expecting the other side would stop me. They didn't. Because I really wanted to do a deal, I had to come crawling back and my power was diminished."

Know your "bottom line"

"I know this sounds obvious, but I'm not sure people always know the point where they would rather walk away than do the deal. Sometimes you may know the bottom line in terms of finance, but haven't established a 'walk away' on the 'soft' issues like how people feel about or value things. If you do know this, make sure your team knows it as well!"

You can fake it for only 15 minutes

"Poker-faced people who try to reveal nothing can't do it for long. The prolonged poker face in itself becomes a comedy. It starts to wear down. Same with people who are too nice, or too aggressive. Don't be too mean or too nice because they are both too hard to fake."

Don't lie

"I interviewed someone for one of our senior manager positions and during the salary negotiations he lied about having other job offers. We couldn't meet his salary expectations, so we moved to another candidate. The original candidate came back to us and it was too late to fix."

If you don't ask, you don't get

"People will let you get away with earning less than you might, or with getting a bad deal. I was afraid if I negotiated I wouldn't get the job. Over the years for me it became a habit not to ask. When I did attempt to negotiate for more pay I was met with 'But you said yes at the interview!' I was good at negotiating the job but not the pay. The responsibility lies with you to ask for what you want."

If you don't rock the boat, you'll go down with the ship

"During a very stressful negotiation with my team and a longstanding client, I realized that we were all agreeing on issues about which I knew we had opposing views. Before my eyes, everyone was resisting conflict at all costs and creating the illusion of agreement. This often happens when individuals in a group are anxious not to rock the boat and therefore collectively decide on a course of action that doesn't represent the preferences of most of them. This is known as the Abilene Paradox and it's something to be wary of."

Know your negotiating partner

"Very few people negotiate up – why is this? Does our fear of missing out mean we would rather negotiate down?

"My husband was a procrastinator and during our divorce there was a high probability that he would never decide what was an appropriate financial settlement. But I knew that I had been fair and ethical in my calculation of the settlement I wanted.

"Therefore my tactic to counter his procrastination was to tell him for every week he delayed the decision to settle I would put my figure up by 10%. It worked. He talked to his friends about my tactic and they all advised him to settle immediately."

Use a "bogey" as a wedge

"Whenever I get ready to buy something significant (I used this on my last refrigerator purchase) I say to the salesman, 'I would love to purchase your product but have only so much money to spend.' By doing that I invite the salesman to help solve my 'budget' problem. Invariably, he gets involved to see how he can help me fit within my budget. The conversation then moves away from any tension of 'what' to 'how' we find a solution together. Kind of 'us against the problem of my budget'. This approach may not necessarily lead to a lower price, but I always learn a lot more, faster, about the product and how flexible they are on price, than if I don't do it."

The phone persona

"One of my counterparties has a reputation for hard-balling deals when he is on the phone. He is very alpha-dog, so I don't even bother to try and have a civilized conversation with him until he has vented his opening position thoroughly. Our telephone meetings start with him interrupting, and talking aggressively and loudly. My initial response is to ask kindly, 'In the spirit of everyone having an opportunity to share their views and ensuring we all have clarity, may one person speak at a time?' Then, 'Thank you for your proposal. I have also prepared some terms that would work for us. I can see we have some different expectations, but I would like to explore how we might make it work.' Cools him down every time."

Write everything down

"Before the negotiation, write down your key issues, your openings, concessions, and walk-aways. During the negotiation, write down what you've agreed and put any ideas or proposals on a flipchart. After the negotiation, write down the final agreements, sign them, and circulate them. Also, be sure to answer any unanswered questions directly – even if they have nothing to do with the deal."

Log rolling: you scratch my back and I'll scratch yours

"Don't think that the person you are negotiating with is automatically and directly opposed to what you are offering. They are likely different, but not opposite. We needed a dog-sitter to look after our house and dogs while we went away for vacation. The sitter was very firm on her hourly wage, but for us the timing was more important. So we were able to come to an agreement that she got her wage and we could be spontaneous about choosing our vacation times. Be firm on what you want and flexible on things that are not so important."

Who, me? Biased?

"People tend to perpetuate and exaggerate their differences if there have been long-standing conflicts. People are people and they choose 'what happened to them or to someone they know' to justify biased actions they take during a negotiation. In my case, having to wade through cultural biases between my Middle Eastern and northern European clients meant it often took us longer to reach agreement on small things. It was as if they preferred to annoy each other as part of the process. We got a lot done when we spent more time just being friendly to each other."

Doing the Doolally

"I used to work for a guy who believed it was useful to have a Doolally on the team. This was someone who was charming, in our case a fairly senior manager, but who purposely said a lot about a little. The result was kind of a smokescreen to divert the other side away from sticky issues, or perhaps buy time for us if we needed to re-group. Once we were asked by our negotiation partners if we would remove him from the team! We didn't, but we asked him to stop talking so much."

If you don't cancel it, assume it's yours

"Read the fine print! During the final settling of the negotiation, we were provided with something we did not agree to (i.e. extra service, extra materials) along with correspondence that made the assumption that we agreed to accept these 'extras'. This placed the burden on us to formally reject them. If we hadn't actively cancelled, the other side would have assumed we agreed. The detail is so important. By the time you realize it, it may be too late."

Be sure the "deadline" is genuine

"Often as a negotiation moves closer to a supposed deadline, the number and the magnitude of concessions increase. Some deadlines are real, others may just be an attempt to push you to make a decision or keep you from being able to plan properly. My advice is: always ask, 'What will happen if we don't meet the deadline?', 'Who exactly is imposing the deadline?', 'Can I change the deadline if it will help us create a better agreement?'"

Don't make deliberate mistakes so that you can "fix" them

"We caught a vendor deliberately signing an agreement before we could see there was a small mistake in it that was in his favor, but contrary to our discussions. Later, we found the mistake and he corrected it. He acted like he was doing us a favor, but it just made us angry."

If you throw a spanner in the works, people will throw it right back

"We had a very powerful client who used to 'test' us during negotiations. He would deliberately mix things up by making last-minute demands or revising product delivery schedules. He thought he would 'catch us out', but because we expected it every time we built in some time and extra resources for ourselves."

Play fair or go home

"I build my personal value of fairness into my negotiating goals and I believe it makes it harder for the other party to play any other way. It's like an 'anchor' for the negotiation. I need to be sure I'm consistent as well and to be aware of any attempts to exploit me. Nine times out of ten it works."

Lift this, then that

"When I went to buy a car, the salesman started our meeting by showing me cars in a particular order, starting with something that was really outside of my criteria (expensive) and then moving on to something more reasonable. If you make an outlandish (but not offensive) initial request, the other side is more likely to give you agreement on the next, smaller request. It's the same as if a person lifts a heavy object, sets it down, and then lifts a light object: they will perceive the light object to be much lighter than it actually is. It's called 'perceptual contrast'."

The squeakiest wheel

"I worked with an art director who had a reputation for drama in meetings. He was dramatic and irrational and once he calmed down he would usually get what he wanted. Not recommended unless you are really good at what you do – and no one is that good! The danger is that people will negotiate around this type of person until one day the drama doesn't work any more. In my case, the clients finally decided they had had enough and demanded he not be involved in future discussions."

Pick up the phone

"I spend a lot of time negotiating with my vendors through email. It's difficult because the face-to-face clues that I rely on are not there. I have found it useful to pick up the phone and talk, because then at least I get their tone of voice. This significantly reduces the likelihood of misinterpretations. So take an opportunity to build the relationship. Find an excuse to call."

Monopoly money

"Particularly when dealing with financial issues, I try to simplify by using percentages or other factors such as man hours, price per unit, price per day/month/year. It helps people who are not numbers-oriented understand, but can really aggravate people who love detail. For example, 'It works out to only 5 cents more per hour' puts the idea into perspective but doesn't focus on the overall costs. I always have to have the real numbers ready."

Good cop–bad cop

"This idea is so familiar to most people that I am amazed when I see it presented to me. This is where two people play two 'roles' – one is aggressive and demanding, the other reasonable and friendly. The most important thing to remember is that the Good Cop is not necessarily on your side."

It takes a village

"I negotiate in a very complex, multi-layered organization. Often there are many people from other countries involved. I find it useful to persuade one or two people at a time and then use them as advocates to persuade others. It makes it easier and I think we end up with a better result."

Plants and leaks (not planting leeks)

"Most of my negotiations predictably come up at about the same time every year. I find both sides 'leak' or 'plant' information as if it is a 'secret' to be discovered. The effect is that it can change expectations or perceptions prior to the negotiation. Lesson: check everything before believing anything. If you think it is an intentional leak, it probably is."

Nibbling away at the deal

"Be prepared for people asking for one last small concession just before signing. We negotiate a lot with people who have English as a second or third language. Sometimes it is cultural, sometimes just hard to finalize details in another language. Nibbling also happens after agreement has been reached. New issues come up, changes are needed, and new people become involved. It helps if you mention your feelings about nibbling at the very beginning of the negotiation, i.e. that you don't take kindly to it."

Padding

"Insert items/issues that are relatively unimportant to you into the negotiation and treat them as 'essential.' Use these items as trade-off concessions to gain agreement on things you really do value."

Red herrings

"Most people think these are deliberate attempts to mislead or confuse. Often they are, but sometimes they arise out of misunderstanding or different perceptions. Always check before you get mad."

Too many aspirations

"I was involved in a negotiation where the other party was enthusiastic and positive but had too many high aspirations. It felt as if they hadn't thought the issues through and we weren't sure which was most important because everything was important. Our response was to be skeptical and we ended up feeling as if we'd "deflated" them in order to get the deal done."

Scarcity

"My experience is that if someone says there aren't many left or that something is exclusive, for the right thing, it cranks up the pressure and the urgency. Items are more valuable to us when their availability is limited. Always verify if something is truly 'scarce' before you believe it. One of my colleagues replied in a negotiation to someone who mentioned scarcity as an issue, 'Unless we are talking about collecting Roman antiquities, I think your product is still only worth its intrinsic value.'"

Negotiating is like dancing

"I prepare like crazy for my negotiations but most of the time I find the other side is neither well prepared nor very good at negotiating. Some people who have a lot of business experience and are known experts in their field surprise me with how little they know about the breadth of issues at stake or how to behave in a negotiation. It is hard to judge how skilled someone is at negotiating in the same way it is hard to tell if someone is a good dancer before the music starts."

Women and men are more equal than they think

"So-called 'slicing the pie' (who gets a bigger slice or does better) in a negotiation depends totally on mindset, not gender. Bring well-prepared and realistic expectations, rather than stereotypes, and both men and women do better."

Never say never unless you mean it

"I made this mistake a couple of times in the middle of a heated negotiating moment. Never is an emotional word, so be careful how you use it."

A bouquet is better than a ball of string

"Whenever possible, handle and discuss several issues or parts of the deal at the same time rather than organize a one-issue-at-a-time, step-by-step agenda. This way you have all the possibilities visible at the same time, making it possible to consider bundles, packages, or combinations. Remember not to give important things away until you are sure all the real issues have been explored."

Most people look for value, not just bargains

"Value means something different to everyone. Our personal perspective on what is most important or valuable influences us more than we realize. Find out what you have in common and how differently you both value the most important issues."

Beware escalation of commitment

"Confidence, high aspirations, and enthusiasm often go hand in hand with emotional attachment to outcomes. It is important to care, just not so much that you lose touch with your ability to create a good outcome for the negotiation. Our team spent six months reviewing a potential acquisition and in the final month the terms had deteriorated badly. Everyone was so excited and committed that they ignored how bad the deal was getting. In hindsight, we should have written down and agreed our walk-away position. Maybe even then it would have been hard to see through all the excitement."

It is easier to hold firm having done the right thing than to defend a dishonorable move

"Doing the right thing pays off, in my experience. You can also sleep better at night. It may be tempting to retaliate or embarrass someone, but just count to ten or sleep on it before you do anything. If in doubt, don't."

You have more power than you think you have

"No one owns power absolutely. It is often in unexpected places and it shifts, changes, and shifts again throughout the negotiation. In my experience, the most obvious power shifts take place with regard to who has information, authority, control over the time or deadline, and how much each party actually needs what the other one has to offer."

I can't get no satisficing

"People who often negotiate together have to work harder to keep from getting lazy and settling quickly for the most tolerable or digestible terms. Sometimes people will do only enough to get by, rather than push for an excellent result. If you don't keep an eye on it, it's easy to set your sights too low – to work just enough to achieve a mediocre goal. I encourage people to prepare as if they were meeting people for the first time. This makes them work extra hard at listening and being objective."

No one said it was bad, so it must be good

"Negotiation is like any skill. You need to get feedback about what was good and what could have gone better. I do this with my team as well as, where possible, the other party. Once, after going back to get feedback after a negotiation, I discovered we had misunderstood an important issue and were able to fix it. Otherwise, we would have never known."

Label feelings, not people

"I learned some big lessons around how to take the heat out of an argument. Sounds old-fashioned, but it works. Instead of 'You are making me so mad' or 'Your offer is silly', I say, 'I am feeling angry or resentful' or 'I am disappointed with the deal terms.' Switching from 'You are' to 'I am' helped me with my personal relationships too! I take responsibility for my feelings and it makes me feel a little less hot under the collar."

You don't have to like everybody

"Sometimes you have to negotiate with people you don't like. It's life. Instead of trying to like them, just behave differently toward them. Perform a random act of kindness. Sometimes you have to build the bridge just to get on. Your feelings are likely to change over time."

Make an effort to collect wisdom and feedback from others. It's fun, humbling, mostly useful, and a good habit to develop.

nine

Closing

I have fought, I have finished, I have remained faithful
2 Timothy 4:7

I am always reluctant to talk about closing as an isolated event in a negotiation or a sale. The truth is, closing starts even before you begin to negotiate and is made up of a series of small agreements and understandings that happen throughout the negotiation. If you play your cards right, these culminate in a mutually beneficial outcome. So, your closing will be dependent on, or at least affected deeply by, the quality of what came before it. Effective communication can deliver a smoother closing.

From the start, as a Nimble Negotiator you have reached out with the intention of understanding the other person's interests and of clarifying issues and objectives. By doing this you can send a powerful spoken and unspoken message of your interest in the values of fairness, understanding, listening, and building rapport. Remember, you have a strong ability to guide the tone of the whole negotiation with your actions.

Respect, empathy, clarity are powerful adversaries. You are not likely to say yes to someone, no matter how clever or well structured their offer is, if they are disrespectful, sloppy, and show no understanding for your point of view. Think about closing your negotiation as you might build a bridge. As the old saying goes, "You can't cross half a ditch."

The light at the end of the tunnel

Finally, as the negotiation continues you see a light at the end of the tunnel. Settling can take place issue by issue and as a result of the whole negotiation. Here are some options you can use to seal the deal:

- Making an exchange, trade off or compromise ("You take this and I'll take that" or "I'll do that if you make sure this doesn't happen again").
- Reaching a contingency agreement (settlement depends on one or more things happening. If not, then there is no agreement).
- Giving to each other what each values most ("You take the orange peel and I'll take the juice").
- Sharing risk/use/rewards ("You can use the car if you help pay for the running costs and insurance").
- Establishing patterns of giving and receiving ("You pay for it this year and I'll pay next year. Then let's re-evaluate").
- Combining issues ("We'll hold off our decision until the other side decides to purchase their new car or not").
- Separating issues ("Their decision to purchase a car has nothing to do with your decision. Let's make it simple and keep the issues separate").
- Selling mutual ideas or vision ("Together and with our combined expertise we can take over the world!").
- Appointing a mediator or arbiter (an arbiter is usually used for commercial or international transactions and a mediator is a neutral third party who settles a non-binding agreement).
- Splitting the difference (50-50 or dividing "down the middle").
- Getting creative. What else is possible? If you knew the answer, what would it be?

A final checklist

Here are some of the most important things to remember about closing:

- Be certain that all issues, no matter how minor, are resolved.

- Leave nothing to chance and as little as possible to the spirit of goodwill.
- Anticipate final-hour blow-ups.
- If someone says no, probe for the underlying reason.
- Pick the right way to say yes while being careful not to push too far.
- Pave the way for future relationships.

Be certain that all issues, no matter how minor, are resolved

One of the ground rules I suggested in Chapter Two was, "Nothing is agreed until everything is agreed." A little sloppiness here can undo a lot of hard work.

I did some work with a small pharmaceutical company which was negotiating a later phase approval with the Food and Drug Administration on one of their products. As anyone who has been involved with drug approvals in the U.S. knows, the process can be complex, lengthy, and tiring for everyone involved. There is a mix of big-sky, high-priority issues as well as many little details that the team needs to stay on top of, sometimes for years. The long and short of this story is that my clients believed they had received approval and went so far as to begin the process of the drug launch. It had to come to a screeching halt a few months later when they found out that they had not reached agreement on a small design element in the packaging. The team had been so focused on getting the big issues settled, they had overlooked a small but important detail. They had not checked on the full extent of what had been approved, or not, before they proceeded. The setback took them another six months to settle. Two simple but expensive lessons learned:

1. Review your notes carefully. When my clients looked back over the files, they realized that they had missed a separate notation about packaging that had never been addressed.
2. Beware of groupthink. The team had been working together for many months on this project and had developed an esprit de corps that resulted in what they called a "shared belief that

someone else was keeping track of the process". In their words, they were "too comfortable and stopped checking each other's work and keeping track of the outcomes of meetings". They were all scientific subject-matter experts and overlooked the project-management details.

Leave nothing to chance and as little as possible to the spirit of goodwill

As a young (and less seasoned) person, I entered into a business arrangement with some fellow entrepreneurs. We had big dreams, energy and enthusiasm, little money yet favorable prospects for growing our business. From the beginning we were working fast and furious and neglected to agree in writing to formal terms of our partnership. We were all good friends and believed in each other and in the spirit of what we were doing. You can see where this is going. A few years later, we had to make crucial decisions about the future of our now larger and more profitable company. We fundamentally disagreed on critical funding issues and had no contracts or terms for the future of the partnership. It didn't end well.

Moral of the story: Leave nothing to chance and as little as possible to the spirit of goodwill. Stay objective, discuss these important issues early, and save a lot of heartache later.

Some negotiations are formalized. This means they have rules; codes of conduct and processes exist. Like buying a house or a car. Usually, the buyer makes the first offer; depending on where the deal is done, there can be rules around whether that offer should be in writing or whether an agent is involved or not.

Other types of negotiation are not so clear. There is more opportunity for "creative interpretation" or improvisation of what is required. If you are not sure about how to go about a particular kind of negotiation, the best thing you can do is ask. If you don't know, don't negotiate.

Here are some things to think about:

- As Sam Goldwyn said, "A verbal agreement is not worth the paper it's written on." Put every possible understanding in writing: how work is to be divided, profits shared, where funding is coming from, how and why the relationship can be terminated.

If the relationship hits a bumpy patch and you want to go your separate ways, there is nothing left you have to agree on and you are all protected.

- If you are being interviewed for a job, don't start negotiating before you have actually been offered it. This is a common mistake. You are in your strongest position when you have been offered a job but haven't accepted it.

- Be sure the people you are negotiating with have the power to make the deal. Don't get stuck with the car salesman who keeps disappearing to talk with his manager. Ask for clarification early and save yourself a lot of time.

- Ask an experienced person who is familiar with a particular type of negotiation before you jump in. For example, the executive director of a local non-profit was preparing to negotiate an annual bulk purchase of some food to serve kids for an after-school program. She cleverly did her homework and asked a local grocery-store owner about how bulk purchases were done and what to expect when she was doing the deal. She learned a lot about the ideal timing for approaching the decision makers, what would be considered a fair request, what volume options she had, and payment particulars. As an added and unexpected benefit she also developed a new relationship that has given her another supporter for her organization.

Anticipate final-hour blow-ups

Sometimes blow-ups at the last minute are used as a tactic to put pressure on the other side or provoke concessions. Usually, unbeknownst to the individuals who make a habit of perpetrating blow-ups, their bad reputation precedes them. As a Nimble Negotiator, you will glean this during your preparation and can anticipate and prepare for it.

Nimble doesn't mean nice. It means that you respect that people sometimes behave badly under pressure. Before you judge, remember that temper can erupt because of the build-up of tension and emotion that is a normal part of negotiation.

Nervousness has a range of disguises and can manifest itself as anything from simply raising an issue that has already been agreed and trying to change it, to introducing a completely new point or an all-out temper tantrum. Be firm, but always check your facts before responding fully.

Conducting negotiations through lawyers, agents, and other intermediaries can make it difficult to interpret the other side's intentions. There is a virtual back and forth between the parties and haggling done through the grapevine!

When we were selling our house in London, we agreed a price and then relied on the lawyers to complete the negotiation and settle details. Closing the sale by a particular date was critical both for us and for the buyers. However, as the deadline came dangerously close, we discovered the lawyers were creating tactical delays over minor details. They had started their own parallel negotiation that put pressure on the deal getting done on time. So we picked up the phone directly to the buyers and finalized the sale ourselves.

Key tip: With all due respect to intermediaries, stay involved in your negotiation beyond the reports and updates you are getting from your lawyer or broker. Where possible (and even when you think it is not possible), talk to your negotiating partners face to face. You may be able to head off some final-hour blow-ups.

If someone says no, probe for the underlying reason

Chapter Four – Managing Tension – has some good ways to uncover resistance and objection. If someone says no at the close of your negotiation, it is good practice to take a step to understand the reasons for it. Why? Because you may learn something useful about what went well or badly during the process of your negotiation. You will learn more about the other person and what their real needs are, setting the scene for a future relationship and opportunities. Finally, you may learn that there has been a misunderstanding or uncover the possibility of exploring another solution. To persuade someone, remember you need to be sure that what you are offering is relevant and addresses their spoken and unspoken needs.

Listen for clues in their resistance. People say no for many reasons. Here are some of the main ones that may crop up at the end of a negotiation:

- The other party doubts whether you can deliver on what you promised (execution).
- He feels time is on his side and there is no need to rush into a decision. He also doesn't want to be pushed into a decision (timing).
- He can't see the value in what you are offering (relevance).
- He thinks he may be better off doing nothing or doing it with someone else (options).
- He doesn't feel you are being fair, transparent or honest (ethics).
- He doesn't think you respect or understand him (identity).

So, negotiation requires that you are effective on a substantive as well as a personal level. If you hear no, be sure you understand the reasons why.

Pick the right way to say yes while being careful not to push too far

Do you always know when it is time to stop negotiating? The short answer is, stop if you are not making progress and you have a better alternative. It's a little harder to know when to stop when things are going well.

Here are some different ways to say yes and their implications:

Answer One: All's well that ends well.
"Yes. This is fantastic! I really appreciate the effort you have put into this deal. I'll make sure this works for you too."

This kind of yes expresses genuine gratitude and acknowledges the other person's efforts. If someone has made you a generous offer you need to acknowledge it. A response like this can strengthen the relationship and may lead to future collaboration.

Answer Two: I'm happy enough. I'm finished.
"Okay. I had set my hopes on doing better, but I'll accept this and make it work. I appreciate your effort. Thank you."

This is a little more guarded. It suggests the other party may have pushed you close to the edge. This kind of response could be useful if your counterparts are taking the deal back to a "third party" for approval. They also know that you are happy enough with the deal to follow through on your agreements.

Answer Three: I'm happy enough. I'd be happier, though if you'd do this one thing for me.
"We've got a deal. Thank you. I'd appreciate it, though, if you could help me with one last thing."

Here you have made it unlikely that you will jeopardize the deal, but have left it open to do a little better. If you say you accept the deal, it turns the extra item you've asked for into just a favor. Rather than ask for more after you have agreed, say at this point that there is something else.

Answer Four: Looking good. The only thing between us and an agreement is...
"This works for me. If you can guarantee full completion by the end of the month, we have a deal."

This is an "if/then" yes. It expresses enthusiasm, but it is a less than full commitment. Importantly, it suggests the negotiations are not over yet. The other side will have to decide if they want to meet that last condition, but at the same time they know you aren't going to surprise them with another one. The last request could be small or large, but at least it is just one issue rather than putting the whole negotiation into question.

Answer Five: Feeling positive, but not sure yet. I would value the time to think about it. Can you do that for me?
"I really want to do this deal, but I'd like to sleep on it."

If you encounter this kind of half-yes, don't get your hopes up because you don't really have a deal yet. It's good to let the other person sleep on their "decision"; however, test it by getting agreement on a deadline for an answer. Overnight will do.

Picking the right way to say yes is also important. Don't be tempted to sound as if you are doing the other side a big favor, or that they "owe you" something as a result.

I had a client many years ago who was proficient at making both a "yes" and a "no" sound like an effort. His specialty was saying either, "Yes… but you owe me" after a long drawn-out pause (often with a sigh), or a "no" that came with a heavy sigh and a shaking of the head as if in disbelief. The challenge here is that the reciprocity principle applies to both giving and receiving. That means, quite simply, that people tend to treat others the way they are treated. If you behave badly, you increase the likelihood of the other party retaliating.

A major investment bank had been trying to obtain work from a prestigious company for many years. Eventually the company agreed to use the bank for a deal and, in order to cement the relationship, the bank agreed to terms that were very advantageous for the company. As a result, the bank's employees left the deal believing that the company now owed them a debt for these terms and would use them again in the future.

However, the company's employees' view was that the bank now owed *them* because the bank had the opportunity to be associated with the company's prestigious name. None of the anticipation and expectation built up on the bank's side after years of "wooing" was matched by the company. Sounds like unrequited love gone even more wrong.

You have to be sure that the other party actually agrees on some level with your "Yes, but you owe me" and be prepared to face the consequences of creating a feeling of indebtedness or guilt. If they don't see it your way, you set yourself up for disappointment. Why not choose to reflect a more grateful, cooperative, and constructive approach and reap the benefits of the reciprocity principle this way?

Pushing too hard is another kind of yes that can backfire on you. I negotiated with one of my newer employees who had requested a move from New York to our London offices. The negotiations started off well, we liked her enough to accommodate the move, but the discussions moved quickly away from salary and timing to her asking for more and more items to be included in her moving and living costs. Her requests began to seem excessive and we went from being excited about the opportunity for her and the company to feeling that it was too hard and that managing it all would be difficult. In the end we decided not to pursue it.

It is important to realize that the only way to improve your own outcomes is to improve the other party's outcomes.

Pave the way for future relationships

If your relationship is to be a continuing one, do not drive the hardest bargain you can. It is important that both sides can live with the outcome of the negotiations, but neither side should feel completely victorious at the expense of the other. Even if you will never negotiate again with these people, your reputation is at stake. If you stay in the workforce, or your industry, you are likely to run into them again. Small things mean a lot, so finish well. A reputation for fairness and decency can be a big help in future negotiations.

Too often negotiations are perceived to be over, when in reality there is still confusion between the negotiating parties. Closing professionally will avoid these misunderstandings. Be patient and make sure you are not going to have an unresolved issue pop up later because you have not nailed down the details. In most Westernized cultures it is a good idea to have your agreements written down and, depending on the complexity, legally recognized. Whether it is a handshake or a document, a hug or a nod of the head, settling is a good thing.

Afterword

I'm relatively optimistic about the future of negotiation. Since I became a teacher and coach over 25 years ago I have seen a small but interesting shift in how people approach it.

Western-style negotiation has traditionally been rational, linear, taking a logical "common sense" approach. But it's been based on achieving the best outcomes for ourselves and our clients, and has largely ignored the benefits of cooperation and collaboration.

Times are changing. Some leading academic, government, non-government, and corporate institutions have begun to look at improving negotiation processes and methodologies. Their approaches are dedicated to finding better ways to solve real-world problems.

The distance between what used to be different worlds is getting smaller. Technology enables us to engage with each other across cultures (within groups and between groups) and geographic divides in completely different ways. International conflicts now demand that negotiators deal with more complex groups, which require more unofficial interactions, flexibility, and creativity to reach understanding.

In other words, negotiating is moving away from "versus" and toward "and".

The challenge is to break through – or rather step out of – current negotiating systems. A system can't fix itself from the inside. We can't negotiate to solve problems or create meaningful outcomes from our own perspective or through the lens of our own understanding.

The best negotiation thinking and experience realizes that we can't gain real understanding and knowledge if we seek it as something independent or external to us. Knowledge and understanding are things we create together and continue to create as we go along.

The next generation of negotiation is about creating meaning, knowledge, and understanding – together. As we negotiate. The process unfolds as we interact.

The Nimble Negotiator is an attempt at the next step you can take toward good negotiation outcomes. Start from where you are, actively seek clarity first, and then move to create an environment for building an optimal outcome through intention and understanding.

Godspeed

Suggested Reading and Browsing List

Albrecht, Karl, & Steve Albrecht. *Added Value Negotiating: the break-through method for building balanced deals.* (New York: Dow-Jones Irwin, 1993, re-released by the authors.)

Babcock, Linda, & Sara Laschever. *Women Don't Ask: the high cost of avoiding negotiation and positive strategies for change.* (New York: Bantam, 2007.)

Cialdini, Robert B. *Influence – the Psychology of Persuasion.* (New York: William Morrow, 1984.)

Erickson, Juliet. *The Art of Persuasion: how to influence people and get what you want.* (London: Hodder & Stoughton, 2004.)

Erickson, Juliet. *Nine Ways to Walk Around a Boulder: using communication skills to change your life.* (London: Kyle Cathie, 2008.)

Fadiman, Clifton. *The Lifetime Reading Plan.* (3rd ed. New York: Harper & Row, 1988.)

Fisher, Roger, & Daniel Shapiro. *Beyond Reason: using emotions as you negotiate.* (New York: Random House, 2005.)

Fisher, Roger, William Ury, & Bruce Patton. *Getting to Yes: negotiating agreement without giving in.* (2nd ed. New York: Penguin, 1991.)

Kahneman, Daniel. *Thinking Fast and Slow.* (New York: Macmillan, 2011.)

Scott, Susan. *Fierce Conversations: achieving success at work and in life one conversation at a time.* (New York: Berkeley, 2002.)

Thompson, Leigh. *The Truth About Negotiations: crack the code and use it with anyone at any time.* (Upper Saddle River, NJ: FT Press, 2008.)

Tolle, Eckhart. *The Power of Now.* (London: Hodder & Stoughton, 2005.)

Ury, William. *Getting Past No: negotiating your way from confrontation to cooperation.* (New York: Bantam, 1991.)

Wheeler, Michael. *The Art of Negotiation: how to improvise agreement in a chaotic world.* (New York: Simon & Schuster, 2013.)

Index

17222847R00069

Made in the USA
San Bernardino, CA
04 December 2014